Zen Wisdom for Christians

of related interest

Practical Zen
Meditation and Beyond
Julian Daizan Skinner
Foreword by Shinzan Miyamae
ISBN 978 1 84819 363 5
eISBN 978 0 85701 321 7

Buddhist Understanding of Childhood Spirituality
The Buddha's Children
Alexander von Gontard
ISBN 978 1 78592 038 7
eISBN 978 1 78450 289 8

Christian Ashrams, Hindu Caves and Sacred Rivers
Christian-Hindu Monastic Dialogue in India 1950–1993
Mario I. Aguilar
ISBN 978 1 78592 086 8
eISBN 978 1 78450 347 5
Part of the Studies in Religion and Theology series

Re-enchanting the Activist
Spirituality and Social Change
Keith Hebden
ISBN 978 1 78592 041 7
eISBN 978 1 78450 295 9

Zen Wisdom for Christians

Christopher Collingwood

Foreword by Father Patrick Kundo Eastman Roshi

Jessica Kingsley *Publishers*
London and Philadelphia

First published in 2019
by Jessica Kingsley Publishers
73 Collier Street
London N1 9BE, UK
and
400 Market Street, Suite 400
Philadelphia, PA 19106, USA

www.jkp.com

Library of Congress Cataloging in Publication Data
Names: Collingwood, Christopher, 1954- author.
Title: Zen for Christians / Christopher Collingwood.
Description: London ; Philadelphia : Jessica Kingsley Publishers, 2018. |
    Includes bibliographical references.
Identifiers: LCCN 2018019351 | ISBN 9781785925726
Subjects: LCSH: Spiritual life--Zen Buddhism. | Christianity and other
    religions. | Zen Buddhism--Relations--Christianity.
Classification: LCC BQ9288 .C65 2018 | DDC 294.3/92702427-
-dc23 LC record available at https://lccn.loc.gov/2018019351

British Library Cataloguing in Publication Data
A CIP catalogue record for this book is available from the British Library

ISBN 978 1 78592 572 6
eISBN 978 1 78450 980 4

Printed and bound in Great Britain

For
my beloved teacher
Father Patrick Kundo Eastman Roshi
with
love, affection and gratitude

Contents

Foreword

As a Christian priest, I have always had a leaning towards contemplative prayer, but it really came alive when I was acting as chaplain to some Benedictine nuns. I attended one of their retreats, where the talks were given by Ruben Habito Roshi, a Zen teacher as well as a practising Roman Catholic. I was startled to discover that my way of prayer was, to all intents and purposes, the same as he described in relation to Zen. After the retreat, I went to see him and I began to practise Zen under his guidance as my teacher, which helped me in my own prayer life.

Sometime later I had a sabbatical, which I spent under the direction of John Daido Loori Roshi, the abbot of Zen Mountain Monastery in New York. Following this rather intensive experience, I met Father Robert Jinsen Kennedy Roshi, a Jesuit priest and also a Zen teacher, and he led me to the point where he gave me Dharma transmission, with authority to teach Zen. This experience of mine demonstrates the age-old truth that Zen practice is simply passed on from one teacher to another.

It was a friend of mine, Dom Donald McGlynn, the abbot of the Cistercian monastery of Nunraw, who had previously introduced me to the writings of Thomas Merton. Merton's own encounter with Zen had enabled me to see that it was possible for Christians also to practise Zen. The journey I began as a practitioner of Zen was, as you might gather, a long one, taking several years.

When I returned to the UK after some years in the USA, I began introducing a handful of people to Zen, and this ultimately led to the establishment of the Wild Goose Zen Sangha, which now has groups all over the country.

One afternoon, I received a phone call from Chris, asking if he could come and see me. That auspicious encounter marked the beginning of a profound relationship between us, with me becoming his teacher, and leading ultimately to my giving him Dharma transmission, in the same way that I myself had been given Dharma transmission by my own teacher, thus continuing the tradition of Zen practice being passed on from one teacher to another. It was on the basis not so much of his academic knowledge at all, but rather of his own lived experience and practice of Zen that Chris was given this Dharma transmission, enabling him to teach others with the Dharma name of *Ryushin*, which means *Dragon Heart*.

I was overjoyed, then, when I heard that Canon Chris was writing this book. He happens to be a very competent Christian theologian who, like me, has found in Zen practice a way that resonates with Christian contemplative prayer. I rejoice wholeheartedly at the publication of this book, as I know that it comes from a thoroughly dependable source, and I am more than confident that it will be a real aid to all, whether Christian or not, who seek to live life in all its fullness, as promised by Jesus in the gospels. But don't just take my word for it. It's best to experience it for yourself. I can promise that you won't regret it!

Father Patrick Kundo Eastman Roshi

Acknowledgments

It would have been very difficult for this book to have been written without the generosity and support of others. I am extremely grateful to my colleagues who make up the Chapter of York (York Minster's governing body) for enabling me to have a period of sabbatical leave to write it: The Very Reverend Vivienne Faull (now Bishop of Bristol), The Reverend Canons Peter Moger and Michael Smith, and Canons Dr Andrew Green, Dr Jules Winkley and Dr Richard Shephard. Other clergy and lay colleagues also willingly took up the slack caused by my absence, especially The Reverend Catriona Cumming, Kathryn Blacker, Vicki Harrison, Susan Hodgson and Hilary Reynolds.

The Diocese of York generously contributed towards the cost of the sabbatical, and I am immensely grateful to the Revd Terry Joyce for the efficient and caring way in which he ensured that the available funds found their way into my bank account.

Many members of the Minster Community expressed a keen interest in the book when they heard that I was going to write it. That interest has been of more profound significance than I suspect they realised, for which I am deeply thankful.

Jules and Leo Winkley graciously offered the use of their cottage on the North Yorkshire Moors for part of the sabbatical. Not only did this provide me with a place where I could focus on writing, it also gave my wife, Sue, and me time and space to be together, something which was made all the more pleasurable by the numerous people who welcomed us into their lives while we were there.

The staff at Jessica Kinglsey Publishers have been nothing but supportive. I am deeply indebted to Dr Natalie Watson (Senior Commissioning Editor), Emma Holak (Senior Production Editor), Claire Robinson (Production Editor), Samantha Patrick and Sean Townsend (Editorial Assistants), Louise Gill (Production Controller) and Kath Mackrill (copyeditor) for their encouragement, advice, efficiency and professionalism.

My first encounter with Zen was through what I read about it as a student. It was only when I later met The Reverend David Barton, who became my spiritual director, though, that I encountered the practice of Zen at first hand. It was he who first suggested that I join him on a Zen *sesshin*, organised by the Oxford Zen Centre at the Carmelite Priory, Boars Hill, in Oxford. The *sesshin* was led by John Gaynor and Sandy Chubb, teachers at the Oxford Zen Centre, who both played significant roles in my early practice of Zen. I am deeply grateful to them.

At around the same time, in a wonderfully synchronistic way, I came across Father Patrick Kundo Eastman Roshi, a Roman Catholic priest and Zen master, who had founded the Wild Goose Zen Sangha in Gloucestershire as part of the international White Plum Asanga, and who became my teacher. Not for one moment had it ever occurred to me that I would one day be a Zen teacher myself, but in 2016 he gave me Dharma transmission, authorising me as just that. I owe him more than I can ever say. His faith, trust and confidence in me, along with his love, compassion, wisdom and generosity, have had a profound influence and impact on me, and continue to do so, and it is with joy and delight that this book is dedicated to him as a mark of my love and respect for him.

As a teacher, I have students to teach. The members of the York Zen Group, however, teach me far more than I teach them. The opportunity of coming to know students through private one-to-one interviews known as *dokusan* is a huge privilege and also profoundly humbling. For all that I have received and continue to receive from them, I am so thankful.

My own family – my children and their spouses – Ben and Roberta, Andrew and Dania, Dominic and Emma, and Teresa and Chris have always been interested in and supportive and encouraging of my practice of Zen as an Anglican priest. I am always stimulated by the conversations we have and look forward to many more. I learn so much from them. Their love and friendship is one of the greatest joys of my life.

Sue, my wife, has been my lifelong companion and friend, as well as being a fellow practitioner of Zen. I learn so much from her, too. The constancy of her love is extraordinary, something that enables her, time and time again, to put the needs of others before her own, as she did in her support of my writing this book. I am as grateful to her for this as I am for everything else. Her love for me is in this book, as is mine for her.

Introduction

A family wedding

When my second son got married a couple of years ago, he and his fiancée invited a good number of their friends, as well as members of their respective families, to join with them in celebrating their marriage. The majority were in their late twenties or early thirties. Like many of their generation, most were uncommitted to following a spiritual path consciously, but all were clearly searching in one way or another. While organised religion held little or no attraction for them, they were far from indifferent to the big questions that life presents to us. Indeed, in some ways, it appeared to be the case that the formal structures of organised religion, whatever shape they took, were themselves something of an impediment, a disincentive, to an open enquiry and engagement with the questions they wrestled with, because the inherited religious traditions were perceived, for the most part, to provide ready-made answers on a take-it-or-leave-it basis. For this reason, so it seemed, such answers were felt to be hollow. In seeking to tie things up neatly, they failed to do justice to the sheer mystery, wonder and ambiguity of life and of our experience of the world. Most important of all, the answers – readily available in the form of doctrines, rituals or codes of behaviour – failed to touch the heart, to awaken in these younger wedding guests the sense that they were really connecting with them, speaking to them, conveying something to them of their deepest truth, opening their hearts to an experience of life that would enable their hearts to dance and sing. By contrast, everything associated with organised religion had about it the smell of death, or worse – in a rather strange way, perhaps – sheer irrelevance.

Questions of religion and spirituality, however, could scarcely have been ignored at the wedding. My son, after all, was brought up in a Christian family, but his bride was a Muslim, her father being Jordanian and her mother Egyptian. As dusk was falling, the happy couple made their vows and exchanged rings as we looked across the River Jordan towards the twinkling lights of Bethlehem, Jericho and Hebron on the other side of the water, and we were reminded – as if we could have failed to have been aware – that this celebration of love, unity and hope was taking place in a part of the world torn apart across the centuries by religious conflict and division. It was my joy and privilege, as an Anglican priest, to conduct the wedding service, which included readings from the Bible, the Qur'an, the poetry of Rumi and Shakespeare, and a Zen poem – *Hokusai Says* – written by a friend of ours, Roger Keyes (2011), which had been read at the ceremony when I received transmission as a Zen teacher.[1] It was clearly very

---

1   The poem can also easily be found on the internet at
     www.habitsforwellbeing.com/poem-hokusai-says-by-roger-keys/

important to my son and daughter-in-law that Zen had a voice at the wedding, too.

After the wedding itself, some 25 of us spent time together for a few days in Petra and then in Wadi Rum, deep in the Jordanian desert. It was here that I found myself being approached by a succession of friends of the newly married couple who wanted to talk. They were intrigued that I was both an Anglican priest and also a Zen teacher. 'How does that work?' was the puzzle for them, not far below the surface. The conversations generally began with questions about Zen and only then moved on to discussions about Christianity. Somehow or other, Zen provided an entrée for conversations about really important questions, about things that really mattered to these young people searching for a path in life, in a way that would not have arisen, I am convinced, had I simply been an Anglican priest alone. As well as being novel, different and intriguing to those who have not come across it before, Zen is undogmatic and both encourages and presents questions – our own life questions – and invites us to discover the answers for ourselves on the basis of experience. There is an openness at the heart of Zen, and it was this approach that seemed so attractive to those with whom I was having conversations.

Christianity and Zen: a little history

It might seem slightly odd to some that it is possible to be Christian and practise Zen as well, especially given the history of the relationship between the two traditions. Indeed, until the middle of the twentieth century it would have been almost unthinkable. The pain of the brutal persecution suffered by Portuguese missionaries and converts to Christianity at the hands of Buddhists in Japan at the end of the sixteenth and beginning of the seventeenth centuries continued to linger in the corporate memory, and grate, long after the event. As is so often the case, the persecution was not purely a religious matter: it resulted from a toxic mixture of religion, politics, economics, misunderstandings, egocentricity and bids for power. Not that it was like this at the outset, though. It is tempting to suggest that it could have been altogether different, but this would be to ignore the fact that everything in our lives is coloured by the particular historical circumstances and situations in which we live. With the passage of time, however, attitudes, perspectives, assumptions – and possibilities – change.

When Francis Xavier arrived in Japan in 1549, his motive was unequivocally to convert people to the Christian faith. It would be a mistake, however, to assume that he lacked any nuance or sophistication in his approach, that he thought he could commend Christianity without first coming to appreciate and affirm those aspects of the host culture where points of contact might be found. He was, for example, personally 'impressed by the elegance of Japanese society and culture', and he clearly endeared himself to the local authorities in Kagoshima, not least to the daimyo or feudal lord, Shimazu Takahisa, by whom he was favourably received (McDaniel 2016, p.19).

Of no little significance, too, was the friendship he struck up with Ninshitsu, the abbot of Fukushoji, a Sōtō Zen monastery.[2] Formed in the Western Scholastic

---

2   Broadly speaking, there are now two schools in Zen: Rinzai and Sōtō. The former grounds its approach primarily in *kōan* study as a means of precipitating awakening, while the latter adopts *shikantaza* – 'just sitting' meditation – as its basis, although in practice there can be considerable overlap between the two.

tradition, Francis Xavier was keen to discuss matters of belief and doctrine with the abbot but made little headway. Nor could he make sense of the seated meditation which occupied much of the monks' time. Whilst the method proposed broadly – but not exclusively, it should be said – in the *Spiritual Exercises* of Ignatius of Loyola, the primary tool through which Jesuits are formed, is that of discursive meditation, going from 'point to point' in reflecting on a topic or scriptural passage,[3] the basis of Zen meditation is that of allowing the mind to be still. Francis Xavier could not understand what they were 'thinking about', as if meditation was predicated on thinking about something in the first place, and although he and Ninshitsu remained friends, it seemed to the Buddhist community that the missionaries were presenting a faith which 'denied validity of all other points of view' (McDaniel 2016, p.22). Disappointed, too, that the Jesuits were uninterested in helping him to establish trade relations with Portuguese merchants, Shimazu Takahisa himself took against them, withdrew his support for the missionaries and forbade conversions under the penalty of death.

The hammer-blow for the Portuguese missionary expansion and, therefore, for any meaningful, fruitful and creative dialogue between different traditions, came in the form of the apostasy committed under torture in 1633 by Father Christóvão Ferreira, the Portuguese Provincial Superior of the Jesuit mission. When Ieyasu Tokugawa became Shogun[4] in 1598, his overriding concern was to

---

3   See Puhl 1951, pp.26–27, for example, and throughout.

4   Although appointed by the Emperor, the Shogun was the *de facto* ruler of Japan, in practice a military dictator.

unify Japan both politically and culturally. Catholicism was considered to be a threat to such unity, potentially subverting the people's loyalty to the Emperor in favour of a foreign Pope. As a result, Ieyasu ordered the expulsion of all foreign Christians in 1614. Ferreira was one of a small group of Jesuits who went underground, and who, after his apostasy, is said to have co-operated with his torturers in eradicating Christianity (McDaniel 2016, pp.27–28).[5] It is these events that provide the backdrop for *Silence*, the novel by the Japanese Roman Catholic author, Shūsaku Endō, which vividly and dramatically portrays something of the bitter nature of the conflict between Christians and Buddhists, as well as the reality of the spiritual and moral dilemmas faced by those experiencing persecution.[6]

Shūsaku Endō's *Silence*

News of Ferreira's apostasy was met with disbelief among the Jesuits. As we are told at the beginning of the novel, he was a theologian of 'considerable ability' (Endō 1996, p.19). *Silence* centres on the determination of three of Ferreira's fictional former students to infiltrate Japan undercover and discover the real story behind Ferreira's alleged apostasy. 'For these three men, Francisco Garrpe,

---

5   Ferreira took a Japanese name and signed himself, 'the resident of the country of Portugal, Chief Bateren (priest) of Japan and Macao, Christóvão Ferreira, reformed in religion and turned an adherent of Zen' (McDaniel 2016, p.28).

6   A film adaptation of the novel, bearing the same title and beautifully directed by Martin Scorsese, was first shown in cinemas in December 2016, and released on DVD in 2017. Masahiro Shinoda had also directed *Silence* in 1971, but it is thought that Endō was not entirely happy with it, especially the ending (Williams 2017).

Juan de Santa Marta and Sebastian Rodrigues,' the narrator declares, 'it was impossible to believe that their much-admired teacher Ferreira, faced with the possibility of a glorious martyrdom, had grovelled like a dog before the infidel. And in these sentiments they spoke for the clergy of Portugal' (Endō 1996, p.26).

As the novel progresses, the plot crystallises around Rodrigues. At the beginning, he and his fellow Jesuits are full of a somewhat naive idealism, and indeed even glory in the prospect of martyrdom themselves. When he sees at first hand the terrible burden of suffering borne by those being tortured and executed, though, his own faith comes under enormous strain. What the authorities require is that Christians spit or stamp on the *fumie*, an image of Christ or the Virgin Mary, as a sign of their renunciation of the Christian faith. Once Rodrigues has been betrayed and taken into captivity, it becomes clear that the fate of others being tortured lies in his hands. He hears moaning and assumes that it is snoring. The devastating truth is revealed to him, though, that the sounds he hears emanate from those being subjected to the *ana-tsurushi*, the hanging in the pit. This torture involved the victims being bound tightly and suspended head first over a pit, often filled with excrement, while a light gash was made around the temple to allow the blood rushing to the head slowly to trickle to the ground, thus prolonging the agony, often for days. Rodrigues's spiritual agony derives from the realisation that until and unless he himself apostatises, countless others will continue to suffer the *ana-tsurushi*. Those hanging over the pit are simply being used as pawns by the authorities to get to Rodrigues; indeed, they have each apostatised several times already. All he has to do to bring the suffering of others to an end is trample on the *fumie* himself.

The climax of the novel is an encounter between Rodrigues and Ferreira. Ferreira explains when they meet that he himself had been in exactly the same situation as Rodrigues finds himself. It dawns on Rodrigues that he 'had believed in his pride that he alone in this night was sharing in the suffering of that man.[7] But here beside him were people who were sharing in that suffering much more than he' (Endō 1996, p.265). Ferreira had prayed with all his might but God had remained silent and done nothing. Ferreira then challenges Rodrigues:

> 'You make yourself more important than them. You are preoccupied with your own salvation. If you say that you will apostatize, those people will be taken out of the pit. They will be saved from suffering. And you refuse to do so. It's because you dread to betray the Church. You dread to be the dregs of the Church, like me.' Until now Ferreira's words had burst out as a single breath of anger, but now his voice gradually weakened as he said: 'Yet I was the same as you. On that cold, black night I, too, was as you are now. And yet is your way of acting love? A priest ought to live in imitation of Christ. If Christ were here... (Endō 1996, p.270)

So it is that the inevitable denouement is reached. As Rodrigues prepares to apostatise by trampling on the *fumie*, he hears Christ himself speak to him: 'Trample! Trample! I more than anyone know of the pain in your foot. Trample!

---

7   i.e. the man 'snoring' in the pit.

It was to be trampled on by men that I was born into this world. It was to share men's pain that I carried my cross' (Endō 1996, p.271). Rodrigues's commission of apostasy is narrated with the utmost sparseness: 'The priest placed his foot on the *fumie*. Dawn broke. And in the far distance the cock crew' (Endō 1996, p.271).

Issues raised by *Silence*

It is part of Endō's genius that he renders us almost mute when attempting to make any judgement about Rodrigues (and Ferreira, too). Did they act out of genuine love in the true spirit of Christ or did they betray him and themselves with him? Was their idealisation of martyrdom born of egocentricity and delusion or was it a mark of genuine selflessness? In T.S. Eliot's play, *Murder in the Cathedral* Archbishop Thomas Becket, in his sermon in Canterbury Cathedral on Christmas Day 1170, muses on the ambiguity of martyrdom:

> A Christian martyrdom is never an accident, for Saints are not made by accident. Still less is a Christian martyrdom the effect of a man's will to become a Saint, as a man by willing and contriving can become a ruler of men. A martyrdom is always the design of God, for His love of men, to warn them and to lead them, to bring them back to His ways. It is never the design of man; for the true martyr is he who has become the instrument of God, who has lost his will in the will of God, and who no longer desires anything for himself, *not even the glory of being a martyr*. (Eliot 2004, p.261; emphasis added)

In a curious way, the predicament of Endō's characters is not entirely dissimilar in character to that experienced by one now revered as a twentieth-century martyr, Dietrich Bonhoeffer. As a Lutheran pastor in Nazi Germany, he came to the conclusion that he could no longer stand by in the face of evil and became involved in a plot to assassinate Hitler, for which he was eventually hanged in Flossenbürg Concentration Camp in April 1945, just days before the end of the Second World War. Was he right to take up violence or would he have been truer to Christ by loving his enemies? Was he actually more Christ-like in letting go of his concern for his own salvation and acting to resist evil or did he compromise his faith?

It is easy for us to adjudicate on such issues at a distance and in the abstract. All of us are faced with real-life decisions and dilemmas on a daily basis. In a review of Martin Scorsese's film, M. Antoni J. Ucerler, S.J., a member of the Japanese Province of the Society of Jesus, makes the following perceptive observations:

At no point does Endō condone or equate apostasy with the 'new normal'. Rather, he concentrates on an understanding of Christian faith marked by suffering and divine mercy. The novel reminds us of a Zen *kōan*, a short, pithy saying that presents the Buddhist novice in training with a seemingly absurd or contradictory statement, whose purpose is to free the mind from the illusion that rationality alone can penetrate the depths of truth. Not everything is black and white. Enlightenment lies elsewhere. (Ucerler 2016)

In suggesting that the film (and, therefore, the novel) is not unlike a Zen *kōan*, Ucerler catches the spirit of both the film and of Zen, for the effect of a *kōan* is first of all to arouse in us a sense of doubt, not for its own sake alone but as the prelude to awakening to reality as it is. Zen rests on the tripod of great faith, great doubt and great determination. The doubt which a *kōan* initially arouses is a doubt, as Ucerler, suggests, that 'rationality alone can penetrate the depths of truth'. Sitting with a *kōan* requires that we stay with the discomfort, the uncertainty, the ambiguity of doubt, and wait for a breakthrough, for a way of seeing things as they really are beyond the casual, superficial, dualistic judgements we habitually make. Importantly, too, we discover that *kōans* are not simply about the people referred to in them; they are about us, our lives, our experience. *Silence*, therefore, is just as much about us as it is about Ferreira or Rodrigues or any of the other characters in the novel. Indeed, Ucerler articulates the unspoken question with which we are all left in one way or another at the end of the film: 'Having set off for Japan thirty-one years ago as a young and enthusiastic Jesuit missionary, I cannot help but be haunted by a simple yet painful question: Had I been born in 1564 rather than 1964 and found myself in Rodrigues's shoes, *what would I have done?*' (Ucerler 2016).

Christianity and Zen: a more positive encounter

It was not quite 400 years after Francis Xavier had first arrived in Japan that another Jesuit, Father Hugo Enomiya-Lassalle (1898–1990), travelled to that same country as a missionary, to study at the Jesuit University of Sophia in Tokyo. By the time Enomiya-Lassalle arrived in Japan, circumstances were somewhat different from those of the sixteenth-century. Enomiya-Lassalle was drawn to Zen and began to study it first with Daiun Sogaku Harada Rōshi (1870–1961) and subsequently with Kōun Yamada Rōshi (1907–1989). Enomiya-Lassalle remained a faithful Catholic priest until his death in 1990, but in 1978, Yamada gave Enomiya-Lassalle transmission, acknowledging him as a Zen master in his own right, thus making Enomiya-Lassalle a pioneering example of what is now referred to as 'dual belonging'.[8] Harada and Yamada were clearly extraordinarily generous in allowing Christians to study with them, not only because they could see how Christians could benefit from the study of Zen, but also because they could appreciate something of the true spirit of Christianity as well. As another Jesuit and later student of Yamada recounted:

> Yamada Rōshi told me several times he did not want to make me a Buddhist but rather he wanted to empty me in imitation of 'Christ your Lord' who emptied himself, poured himself out, and clung to nothing. Whenever Yamada instructed me in this way, I thought that this Buddhist might make a Christian of me yet! (Kennedy 2007, p.14)[9]

---

8   See more on this, for example, in Cornille (2010) and Drew (2011).

9   Ruben Habito also studied with Yamada and speaks about both him and his own experience of self-emptying in the spirit of Christ in Habito (2017, pp.172–187, especially pp.174 and 181).

What a far cry this was on both sides from the early encounters between Christians and Buddhists in the sixteenth and seventeenth centuries!

Nostra aetate

If the initial encounter between Christianity and Zen at that stage, though, was fraught with misunderstanding, suspicion and conflict, the last 70 years or so have witnessed the gradual blossoming of a wonderfully generous, ecumenical hospitality in many quarters. Encouragement for this was provided by the Second Vatican Council in the first half of the 1960s. In particular, a deceptively short document, *Nostra aetate* (28 October 1965), subtitled, 'Declaration on the Relation of the Church to Non-Christian Religions', although only a mere 1600 words in length, had mind-blowing repercussions.

Part of what lay behind *Nostra aetate* was an acute and painful awareness of the sometimes appalling treatment of Muslims and Jews by Christians over the years. The Second Vatican Council was concerned, therefore, to repudiate unequivocally any instances of persecution and to reprove 'as foreign to the mind of Christ, any discrimination against people or harassment of them on the basis of their race, colour, condition in life or religion' (Flannery 2014, p.574).

The first part of the document, totalling less than 600 words, addresses the Church's relationship with oriental religions, specifically Hinduism and Buddhism. Beginning by affirming the common humanity of all people, it expresses appreciation of the fact that all religions seek in their distinctive ways to provide the context for an exploration of humanity's deepest questions about life and the 'ultimate mystery, beyond human explanation, which embraces our entire existence, from which we take origin and towards which we tend' (Flannery 2014, p.570). It acknowledges the value of 'profound meditation and recourse to God in confidence and love' found in Hinduism, and in the case of Buddhism affirms that in its various forms it 'testifies to the essential inadequacy of this changing world [and] proposes a way of life by which people can, with confidence and trust, attain a state of perfect liberation and reach supreme illumination either through their own efforts or with divine help' (Flannery 2014, p.570). While the document asserts that the Church is 'duty bound to proclaim without fail, Christ who is the way, the truth and the life', it also affirms that the 'Catholic Church rejects nothing of what is true and holy in these religions', since although they differ in many ways from the Church's own teaching, they 'nevertheless often reflect a ray of that truth which enlightens all men and women' (Flannery 2014, pp.570–571).

The impact of this declaration was to give sanction to the many Catholic missionaries, like Enomiya-Lassalle, who were already tentatively engaging in dialogue with people of other faiths, now to do so wholeheartedly. Thus in India, people like Henri le Saux (1910–1973), a French Benedictine monk who later adopted the Sanskrit name Swami Abhishiktānanda, and Bede Griffiths (1906–1993), an English Benedictine monk who took the name Swami Dayananda, explored Hinduism from within, while retaining their Christian convictions and commitments.[10]

---

10 For their own accounts see, for example, Griffiths (1976, 1982) and Abhishiktānanda (1975, 1976, 1984).

In the case of Zen, it is remarkable to note, given the history already referenced above, the prominence of Jesuits in this regard, indicating a real spirit of charity and reconciliation as well as genuine curiosity and enquiry. A key figure in this movement was Father William Johnston, S.J. (1925–2010), who worked for many years as a Professor of Oriental Religion at Sophia University in Tokyo, and who did much to make known to the Western world the riches and delights of Zen. Although Johnston did not himself take the step of receiving transmission as a Zen master, others did, notably Father Robert Kennedy S.J. (b.1933), Father AMA Samy S.J. (b.1936), Ruben Habito (b.1947) and Sister Elaine MacInnes (b.1924).[11]

Dialogue for people such as these meant not simply debating with those from other traditions at a cerebral level but really entering into the heart and spirit of other faith traditions. Whereas the initial impetus for dialogue on the part of Christians might have been for the purpose of converting others, what emerged in the process was a recognition that genuine relationships could not proceed on the basis of dominance or superiority but on the basis, rather, of humility, respect and love. Above all, there grew a sense of mutuality, an awareness that each has something of tremendous value to share with and offer to the other, in such

---

11   For representative examples of their work, see Johnston (1970, 1971, 1978, 1981), Kennedy (2004, 2007), Samy (2009, 2010, 2012, 2016, 2017), Habito (2004, 2013, 2017) and MacInness (1999, 2003). Although Habito began practising Zen as a Jesuit priest, he was subsequently laicised and married. He still continues to practise Zen as a Roman Catholic, though, and clearly values the tradition in which he was first formed, as is witnessed by his book, *Zen and the Spiritual Exercises* (2013). For secondary material on Habito and others, see Drew (2011, pp.21–38) as well as McDaniel (2016).

a way that both are enriched and enlarged. For this to happen, what is required is humility and a willingness to listen to and learn from others in a spirit of complete openness.

Boundless openness

'Boundless openness' is how AMA Samy, the contemporary Jesuit Zen master living in India, describes the characteristic stance of Christians who practise Zen. Such openness, however, takes us into the heart of the Christian Paschal mystery, for it demands that a Christian 'must learn to let go, to pass over, to die, into Zen and Zen tradition. Having died, he/she can come back to life'. For dialogue to be 'genuine and life-giving, it must be a passing over and dying into the other…Then Zen will reveal Christianity to the Christian and Christianity reveal Zen to the Buddhist' (Samy 2009, p.121).

This does not imply a syncretistic mixture of bits of this and bits of that, though. Rather:

> one is both at home and grounded in one's original home as well as in the other into which one has passed over. Or better, one stands in the in-between. Christianity is absolutely and fully true, and Zen is absolutely and fully true. At the same time, Christianity is being transformed by Zen, and Zen is being transformed by Christianity. The heart of Christianity is discovered as boundless openness to the other, and so also Zen is realised as openness to Christianity. But not inter-mixed nor harmonised nor synthesised; rather, it is the person standing in the in-between whose heart and mind have been opened up as boundless openness. It is neither relativism nor

pluralism. Each is unique, irreplaceable and absolute. Conflicts and contradictions will still be there, but it is a dynamic and creative tension. Christianity embraces all of reality, and Zen embraces all of reality. It is a divine paradox; there is no use in trying to explain in clear logical terms and one has to live in unknowing and mystery. A helpful metaphor may be the understanding in physics of the electron now as wave and now as particle. But it is in the praxis of passing over and returning that one realises and lives out the mystery. This is the mystery of Christ Jesus. (Samy 2010, pp.201–202)

Openness can be a scary and risky business, but it is in no small measure what makes us more fully human. We are living at a time when, globally, boundaries and limits, particularly political ones, are now being redrawn, hardened and set, where openness in some degree or other had hitherto been taken for granted. The reasons for this are many and varied and it is far beyond the scope of this book to attempt an explanation, even if it were relevant in this context. It is probably the case that we all veer back and forth, first in this and then in that direction. When we feel we are out of our comfort zone, we pull back; when we feel constrained and constricted, we push at the boundaries in search of greater openness. Something that can help us to understand this is brain neuroscience, and Bede Griffiths can provide us with a particular route into this field.

The two hemispheres of the brain

When Bede Griffiths set sail for India in 1955, he was in search of something that he felt was lacking in the Western world and in the Church. He described his journey as being about finding the other half of his soul:

> We were living from one half of our soul, from the unconscious, rational level and we needed to discover the other half, the unconscious, intuitive dimension. I wanted to experience in my life the marriage of these two dimensions of human existence, the rational and intuitive, the conscious and unconscious, the masculine and feminine. I wanted to find the way to the marriage of East and West. (Griffiths 1982, pp.7–8)

At the time, he understood these two dimensions as corresponding to the different functions of the two hemispheres of the brain. He was undoubtedly correct in general terms in drawing attention to the nature of the brain to account for what he perceived to be an imbalance in the Western world and Church, even if his understanding of the particularities of the two hemispheres has now been superseded by further research.

In his ground-breaking book, *The Master and his Emissary*, Iain McGilchrist suggests that for human beings there are 'two fundamentally opposed realities, two different modes of experience; that each is of ultimate importance in bringing about a recognizably human world; and that their difference is rooted in the bihemispheric structure of the brain'. He argues, furthermore, that the two hemispheres need to co-operate with each other but that they are 'involved in a sort of power struggle, and that this explains many aspects of contemporary Western culture' (McGilchrist 2010, p.3).

Building on research into the bipartite structure of the brain in animals and birds, he proposes that humans attend to the world in two different ways. The right hemisphere 'underwrites breadth and flexibility of attention, while the left brings to bear focussed attention'. As a result, the right hemisphere 'sees things whole, and in their context, where the left hemisphere sees things abstracted from context, and broken into parts, from which it then reconstructs a "whole": something very different'. Importantly, the 'capacities that help us to form bonds with others – empathy, emotional understanding, and so on – which involve a quite different kind of attention to the world, are largely right-hemisphere functions' (McGilchrist 2009, pp.27–28).

McGilchrist's thesis, not at all unlike that of Griffiths, is that the Western world has become dominated by the left brain. It is not that the left brain has no place, far from it. It is rather that the domination of the left brain leads to an imbalance in our experience of the world. The left brain, after all, is the Master's Emissary, but it is the right brain that is the Master. In addressing the question of how balance might be restored, McGilchrist suggests that we might learn from oriental culture and, in particular, from the Japanese:

> The sharp dichotomy in our culture between the ways of being of the two hemispheres, which began in Ancient Greece, does not appear to exist, or at any rate, to exist in the same way, in Oriental culture: their experience of the world is still effectively grounded in that of the right hemisphere.
>
> The Japanese also preserve a healthy scepticism about language, and this goes hand in hand with the rejection of

a reality that must, or ever could, be arrived at purely by reason. In Zen Buddhism, according to Soiku Shigematsu, the abbot of Shogenji temple, 'a word is a finger that points at the moon. The goal of Zen pupils is the moon itself, not the pointing finger. Zen masters, therefore will never stop cursing words and letters'. (McGilchrist 2009, pp.452–453)

This might help to explain the increasing attraction of Zen to some Christians, for the practice of Zen engages the right brain's way of attending to the world. The contemplative attitude towards the world, for which a place could certainly be found until the sixteenth century in the Western world, was seriously impaired by the Reformation, and while there have been many benefits arising from the Reformation and all that it precipitated, one of its legacies is an imbalance and distortion in the way we attend to the world. My own experience is that if Zen is practised on its own terms and for its own sake, rather than simply as a means to something else, the whole of life is experienced in a new way. There is an appreciation of difference, a restoration of balance, and an experience of wholeness. The Christian faith, too, comes alive in hitherto unexpected ways. It is in that spirit that this book is offered.

PART 1

Raising the
Bodhi Mind

Chapter 1

A Sense of Exile

Looking in from the outside

I remember visiting the website of a Zen centre some years ago. Included in various bits of video footage on the site was a section of what took place in the *zendo* or meditation hall. *Zabutons* and *zafus* – mats and cushions – were to be seen around three walls of the *zendo*, and against the centre of the fourth was a table with a statue of the Buddha on it. Apart from these and one or two other items, the whole room was wonderfully uncluttered. People were seen entering the *zendo* one or two at a time, pausing at the entrance, where they placed their hands together in *gassho* – what many people would recognise as the classic prayer posture – with both hands held flat against one another in an upright position. After bowing in the direction of the Buddha, they made their way to their places, to which they also bowed before sitting down. A bell was struck three times and there followed complete silence.

Seated meditation – *zazen*, as it is called in Zen – more often than not takes place in 25-minute chunks. What was shown on the website was scarcely more than five minutes or so, but the effect was extraordinary. The camera went around the *zendo* slowly, passing by each person, who could be seen sitting completely still, their hands placed in their laps in the *cosmic mudra* position, which is to say: the left hand placed over the right with the palms facing upwards, and with the thumbs lightly touching each other in the middle, thus making an oval shape. The eyes of each person were half open and the gaze was directed to the floor a short distance in front of them. Light streamed in through the windows and, with the exception of a curtain rustling in a gentle breeze, everything and everyone in the room was quite still. Above all, there was a sense of peace and calm, a quality of silence which is rarely encountered these days, and this atmosphere was almost tangible.

Although I had been practising meditation for some considerable time, I can remember reacting in two ways to what I was watching. On the one hand, it all seemed terribly familiar, comforting even, and there was a feeling of being at home with it. This, after all, was something I did every day. On the other hand, I recall catching myself thinking how odd it seemed and feeling momentarily a sharp and unexpected sense of discomfort, of alienation. It occurred to me that anyone visiting this website, never having experienced meditation, could have been forgiven for thinking that this was one of the most bizarre scenes imaginable, and such apparent oddness would more than likely have provoked a whole torrent of questions: What on earth are they doing? Why are they just sitting there doing nothing? Isn't it incredibly boring? What's the point of it? What purpose could it possibly serve?

So what had drawn the people seen in that video to Zen? Why did they meditate? Given everything that goes on in the world and in our lives, the pain and the suffering, the distress and the heartache, the anger and the frustration, the bitterness and the hatred, the malice and the violence, why would anyone respond to all that by simply stopping, sitting still and doing nothing, when there's so much that needs to be done?

One possible answer, of course, would be that they were simply running away, as could be the case with everyone who meditates. Meditation, after all, must appear to some to offer a lovely way to escape the burdens, the stresses and the demands of life, even if only for a few minutes each day. Various forms of meditation are indeed promoted as aiding relaxation and helping to relieve stress and anxiety among other things. Even if someone is drawn to the practice of Zen in the first instance by such expectations, sooner or later it comes to be realised that, even though the relief of stress may sometimes or habitually be a by-product of Zen meditation, this is not the primary motivation for practising Zen. Zen is far more than this.

Getting a taste of Zen

What Zen really is can be tested out right now in a very simple exercise. In a moment, I shall invite you to put the book to one side, but first, here are a few necessary instructions. If possible, find somewhere quiet to sit. Make yourself comfortable, sitting, preferably, on a fairly deep and firm cushion on the floor or on a stool or a hard-backed chair without actually resting your own back against the chair. If you are unable to sit because you are confined to bed or because you have to stand for whatever reason, that does not matter. The important thing is to be relaxed, alert and attentive.

When you start in just a minute or two, take a few deep breaths and be aware of the sensations of your body. Notice the rise and fall, the inhalation and the exhalation of the breath, and for a few moments just breathe. There is no need to force anything; just let the breathing be the breathing. After a while, you might notice various thoughts arising. Initially, these might seem to be fairly trivial. They may relate to what you were doing before you began reading this book or you may find yourself remembering something you have forgotten to do. Alternatively, you might begin to notice that you are hungry or tired or that you have a physical ache, itch or pain somewhere. Just let such thoughts come and go, and continue to be gently attentive to the breath. There is no need to feel that these thoughts have to be suppressed.

It might well be that a sense of calm begins to emerge. If so, be grateful but avoid the temptation to hang on to it. If it continues, just notice it and let it be, all the while paying attention to the breath. If disturbance arises, again just come back to the breath and focus your attention on it.

We are nearly ready to begin. Decide on how long you intend to spend on this exercise – 5, 10, 15 minutes or more – and stick to that commitment, whatever happens. If you have a mobile phone, set a timer to sound to bring the exercise to a close at the designated time. All you have to do is pay attention to the breath. If your mind wanders, bring it gently back to the breath. So, put the book to one side and begin, simply noticing what happens, and then, when you have finished, begin reading again.

Reflecting on the experience

Whatever occurred during this brief exercise is simply what happened. There may well be a temptation to make a judgement about it, but resist that; it was simply your experience. Let me suggest some possible scenarios, however, and see whether they resonate with your experience in any way at all. If not, it does not matter.

As you sat with the breath, you might have been aware of thoughts arising which caused you emotional or psychological discomfort. Perhaps you had had a row with someone earlier or you are living with a relationship which is a continual source of tension. You might have experienced disappointment recently, perhaps at work or socially. There might have been a sense of anxiety around, due to ageing or increasing infirmity or uncertainty about money or some such thing. At a deeper level, feelings of frustration, anger or hatred might have surfaced as a result of things like abuse, intimidation or bullying in the past or in the present. If you are a person of faith, you might have found doubts arising or thoughts and emotions which are considered to be unacceptable. If anything vaguely like this was the case, the response is always to let such things come, notice them, and let them go, all the while returning to the breath.

After a while, you might have found yourself questioning what the purpose of this exercise was at all. You could have simply felt bored and longed to bring it to an end. Deeper questions might have emerged, though, questions like: Who is it who is sitting here with thoughts coming and going? Who am I? What is my life all about? Where is God? Is there a God? Why am I so unhappy? What is the purpose of my life? Is there any purpose to anything? Again, the response at every turn to such thoughts is not to resist them but simply to let them be and come back to the breath.

If this is the first time you have done anything like this, you might have been surprised to discover what was going in your mind. The experience might have been overwhelmingly pleasurable for you, bringing a sense of peace, contentment and joy. Perhaps there were few thoughts and time seemed to be suspended. Alternatively, you might have been rather dismayed by thoughts that arose and feel reluctant to try something like this again.

If you are an experienced meditator, then you probably will not have been at all surprised by whatever occurred. Over time we discover, both in times of meditation and in all other circumstances of life, that life is surprising, that we are a mystery to ourselves, that things are not always, if ever, very much in our control, and that we are always more than who we think we are and, indeed, very much more than our thinking itself. Little by little, we learn to let things be, whether they be disturbing or delectable, and try not to become too attached to them.

Coming face to face with ourselves

Whatever you might have experienced in this brief exercise, the important point is this. It might be thought that meditation is about finding a sense of relief from the pressures of life, even escaping, indeed, from what we find difficult and unpalatable. Just sitting in silence for a few minutes, however, brings us to the inescapable and incontrovertible fact about us, which is this: *we cannot escape from ourselves*. The practice of Zen is orientated to one thing and one thing alone: to enable us to see into our true nature and to awaken to who we truly are. My experience of visiting the website as described above revealed to me something that we all know deep in our hearts, whether we are conscious of it or not: that we are not truly at home with ourselves, that we feel alienated and estranged from who we truly are. It is this realisation, and the desire to find out what lies at the bottom of it rather than seek to run away from it, that marks the beginning of the spiritual quest. In Zen terms, this is referred to as 'Raising the Bodhi Mind', which is about responding to the intuitive aspiration to wake up to who we truly are. Another way of putting it is to say that we seek to come out of exile and come home to ourselves, to who we truly are. And the curious paradox is that we do this by 'doing nothing'.

Human experience of life is that it is not what we expect or should like it to be. We dream of something different. We see colossal suffering on a global scale in the form of war and conflict. There are so many seemingly innocent casualties in the bids for power and domination among those who seek political influence and authority among the nations. Millions live in unimaginable poverty, where daily life consists of a battle against disease and starvation. Others have been displaced from their homes and find that they have nowhere to go and no one who wants to give them refuge. Injustice prevails in all sorts of shapes and sizes.

Few, if any, are free from conflict of some kind in their personal lives. Relationships can be difficult. Commitments made in good faith can sometimes prove difficult to sustain, and what follows, apart from the breaking up of a relationship itself, can be the loss of trust in people and in human nature itself. We all bear the wounds and scars of the actions, attitudes and behaviour of others, not least when we were children, although being hurt by others seems to continue into the present, whatever stage of life we may have reached. Nor are we ourselves innocent. Consciously or unconsciously, we often act from the desire to inflict pain on others, which simply adds to the cycles of violence, dysfunction and unhappiness.

It is not surprising that we protest against a general state of affairs which seems to be so unsatisfactory. We feel in our bones that this is not how things should be. For some, it is this very unsatisfactoriness which numbs them to the possibility of any alternative and, therefore, of even seeking something more bearable and fulfilling. Cynicism becomes the default response to life, characterised, perhaps, by an attitude of, 'eat, drink and be merry, for tomorrow we die'.[1] For others, the desire to avoid the pain of living prompts them to seek refuge in that which temporarily relieves pain, but after the effects have worn off, that from which relief was sought is still felt, in most cases all the more strongly, leading often to a sense of despair. Intoxicants of one kind or another initially promise this kind of relief, but we can also escape by means of sex, working far too hard, manipulating relationships, indulging in power games, and much more. However much such things might seem to present ways of dealing with the unsatisfactoriness of life, what remains is a gnawing sense that we are not truly at home with ourselves or with life.

---

1 This saying is a conflation of two biblical verses: Ecclesiastes 8.15 and Isaiah 22.13b.

The search for awakening

In some cases, however, the dissatisfaction with life is itself the means by which we are propelled into the search for awakening. Of course, how people actually choose to respond to tragedy in their personal lives and elsewhere, for example, is more often than not unpredictable. For some, betrayal, or the diagnosis of a terminal illness, or the unexpected and sudden death of someone they love lead to a closing in on themselves. While this is almost certainly an instinctive response, motivated by a desire to protect and defend themselves against such pain ever again, it often leads to bitterness and resentment – towards others, God or just life in general. While such a response is understandable, the effect is to arrest the onward flow of life, and such people get left behind as everything else inevitably and unavoidably moves on, leaving them diminished in all sorts of ways.

In other cases, though, there can be a quite different reaction. The shocking news that a partner, child or friend has been suddenly and unexpectedly killed in an accident, for example, can lead to a questioning of life and its purpose in such a way that opens them up rather than closes them in on themselves. Far from hardening them, as might sometimes be expected, such an experience seems to break them open to new possibilities, to new ways of seeing the world and living in it.

It need not be tragic incidents and experiences alone, which thrust us into a search for something more satisfactory, though. Sheer boredom with our lives, a sense of *ennui*, can serve mysteriously to wake us up. It is not unheard of, for example, for someone who has been following a particular career path and who, to all intents and purposes, appears to be content with it, to give it all up quite out of the blue in pursuit of something different, because the point has been reached where life has lost its spark, its zest, and is no longer satisfying. For many, the temptation simply to put up with the *status quo* is overwhelming, the prospect of change, especially at the expense of a comfortable lifestyle, perhaps, being just too demanding. For others, however, it is precisely this dissatisfaction which initiates the search for what is truly satisfying and life-enhancing. In Zen terms, this is the raising of the Bodhi Mind.[2] It is the response to an inner call to come out of exile and return home.

The Prodigal Son as a story of exile and homecoming

Turning specifically to the Christian tradition, the whole Biblical narrative can be read as a story about humanity's sense of exile and journey home. In particular, Jesus' celebrated parable, known as the Prodigal Son, captures a variety of nuances in our experience of exile and coming home. The story will be well known to many. The younger of two sons, knowing that he will eventually inherit his father's property, is impatient and demands his half share right away. The father responds to his son's insensitivity without question and gives him just what he wants. The son, no doubt believing he now has everything he had ever wanted or needed to make him happy, sets off on a journey far away from home, indeed to a 'distant country', where he squanders his inheritance in reckless and dissolute living. Having run out of money, and

---

2   Zen Master Dōgen, for example, exhorts his hearers to 'arouse the mind that seeks the Way' (Masunaga 1971, p.84).

experiencing famine in that country, he realises he needs to work, and so, as a last resort, so it seems, he accepts work doing the only thing on offer: looking after pigs in the fields. Although this is not spelled out in the parable, we might take it for granted, perhaps, that the son is Jewish, for whom pigs would be considered to be the dirtiest animals around, and for whom contact with which would make him, like every other Jew, ritually unclean, thus emphasising just how low he has sunk, how far from home he has travelled.

It is precisely at this point, though, when he is at his lowest ebb and feeling sorry for himself, when he realises just how far from home he is, that there is an awakening. Reality impresses itself on him and, we are told, 'he came to himself'. Realising his foolishness, he begins to make his way back home, all the while rehearsing in his own mind the speech he intends to give his father, expressing sorrow, regret and shame at having turned his back on him. No longer does he expect to be reinstated to his place in the family as a son, but intends to request that he be treated as no more than a hired servant. None of this, however, is necessary, for the father sees not the errors and misdeeds of his son, but only the person he adores and loves with all his heart. The son who was dead is alive, the one who was lost is found. The exile has come home. There are no recriminations, only celebrations.

Meanwhile, the elder, dutiful son, who has never left home in the way that his brother did, is attending to matters of his father's land and property by working in the fields. On hearing the celebratory music and dancing and the reason for them, his reaction is one of anger and resentment. When he protests that unlike his brother, who has devoured his share of the inheritance with prostitutes, he himself has worked like a slave for his father, never disobeyed one of his commands, nor at any time been given the opportunity to invite his friends round for a party, the father's response is wonderfully eirenic: 'Son, you are always with me, and all that is mine is yours. But we had to celebrate and rejoice, because this brother of yours was dead and has come to life; he was lost and has been found' (Luke 15.31–32).[3]

Drawing out the significance of the parable

This story is rich in meaning and it is worth lingering for a moment to appreciate some of its import. What we would do well to notice at the outset is the younger son's grasping, demanding attitude. It is not hard for any of us to identify with this. In many ways, it appears to be the default attitude of humanity. It springs from the ego, which always seeks to serve itself and its own narrow perspective on life, and its action in this case, as it is invariably, is divisive: it separates the younger son from his father.

Significantly, the younger son fails to recognise that he is already truly at home and believes he lacks something – his share of his father's inheritance – that will make him completely happy, and so, paradoxically, he demands what is already and always his, if only he knew it. This grasping and demanding attitude leads him to travel far away from home, to a 'distant country', alienated from his father, his brother and himself. This distance from home results in his forgetting who he really is and where

---

3   The full text of the parable is to be found in Luke 15.11–?

he has come from, his origin, symbolised at a superficial level by turning his back on his own Jewish heritage. It is the experience of inner division and separation, however, which wakes him up to himself. His familial relationships and his geographical home represent his metaphorical home, his true self, the self that is in harmony with and embraces everyone and everything. In awakening to himself, he recognises home, in the form of his father, to be utterly gracious, compassionate and loving. In this sense, 'exile' is embraced by and contained in 'home'.

It has to be said, though, that the elder son neither appreciates home, nor does he wake up to the truth about home. For him, life seems to be routine and rather mechanical, lived without awareness and characterised by greed and envy. Like his younger brother, he fails to recognise the true nature of home, that there is no need to grasp at anything because he already possesses it: 'Son, you are always with me, and all that is mine is yours'. The tragedy and the irony is that while the younger son has come home, the elder brother is still in exile without realising it.

Quite why we turn our backs on our true home and choose to live in exile is a profound mystery. There are attempts to explain this theologically, of course, but in the end, none seems to satisfy completely. This is why stories are invariably more helpful than abstract explanations. The story of the Prodigal Son, after all, 'speaks' in ways we cannot fully understand ourselves, which is precisely why it is so evocative. It simply rings true to our experience, to our sense of homelessness and our longing for home.

The Bible as a story of exile and homecoming

In many ways, this is the essence of the whole Biblical story, of which the Prodigal Son can be read as a kind of distillation. In the two creation stories at the beginning of Genesis, the Bible begins with a depiction of harmony at every level of creation, which derives from the fact that everything depends for its being on God and is in its proper relation to God. God, humanity, the natural world and the whole cosmos are at one with each other. This harmony, however, is disrupted in chapter three, in the familiar story of the Fall. In the mythological Garden of Eden, everything is rosy until the serpent comes on the scene. The snake tempts the woman to eat of the fruit of the tree in the middle of the garden, the only thing which has been prohibited by God, since eating this fruit will cause a person to die. The serpent rationalises with the woman that this prohibition has been made only because when it is disregarded and the fruit is eaten, her eyes will be opened and she will be like God, knowing good and evil.

The serpent successfully seduces the woman into eating the fruit, whereupon she takes the fruit, gives it to her husband, and they eat, at which point their eyes are indeed opened and, for the first time, they know themselves to be naked. When God is heard walking in the garden in the evening breeze, they hide from fear, and after some questioning, God curses the serpent, decrees that as a result of the act of disobedience the woman will experience pain in giving birth and will be subjected to her husband, and declares that the man will experience work as a hardship. Finally, God banishes the man and the woman from the garden and places an angel and a flaming sword to guard the way to the tree of life. They have been thrown out of their home and cast into exile.

What is going on here? What is this story getting at? As was the case in the story of the Prodigal Son, everything begins to go wrong with an attempt to grasp at something – in this case the fruit. Just as the two sons in the parable discover that there is no need to grasp at anything at all because everything is already theirs anyway, so the man and the woman fail to realise that everything is already theirs, too.

What about the tree in the middle of the garden, though? That is not theirs, is it? Here the narrative is extraordinarily subtle. It is true that the man and the woman have been commanded by God, 'You may freely eat of every tree of the garden; but of the tree of the knowledge of good and evil you shall not eat, for in the day that you eat of it you shall die' (Genesis 2.17). It would be easy to miss something terribly significant here. We read later on in the story that eating of the fruit of the tree is said to make the man and the woman like God (Genesis 3.4), knowing good and evil, but what we often fail to notice is that it is not God who actually says this but the *serpent*. All they are told by God is that eating the fruit of the tree of the knowledge of good and evil – the fruit of duality – will cause them to die, not that this will make them like God.

Within the context of the whole biblical narrative, there is a certain dramatic irony here. Although there are two creation stories at the beginning of Genesis, they are clearly intended to be read as complementary, the second in light of the first, and not in opposition. That is presumably why they were both included, despite various differences and contradictions. The reader knows, therefore, that in the first creation story, it has already been asserted that human beings are created in the image and likeness of God: 'Then God said, "Let us make humankind in our image according to our likeness"… So God created humankind in his image, in the image of God he created them; male and female he created them' (Genesis 1.26a & 27). From the perspective of the whole, the man and woman have no need to become like God for they are already like God, even though in the context of the second creation story they have no way of knowing this for themselves yet. What the reader knows, however, is that eating the fruit, far from making them like God, would do the opposite, for God is beyond duality.

This brings us to the significance of the serpent. The serpent is crafty, so the implication of this passage is that the serpent *misleads* the man and the woman into thinking that it is the eating of the fruit of duality that will make them like God. In other words, the serpent is a trickster, a deceiver, and it is the serpent who tricks the man and woman into falling into a world of separation and duality. When God confronts the woman with what she has done, she responds by saying, 'The serpent tricked me, and I ate' (Genesis 3.13b). The divine prohibition against eating the fruit is not because it will make them like God: they are that already. Rather, it stands as a warning against the possibility of falling into duality, a state in which we are separated from our divine ground, divided against ourselves and everything and everyone else. Falling into duality is precipitated by the bid to be a separate self, and this is the reason why we are in exile, away from home, out of joint and living in a state of dis-ease, of disharmony. As a result, we long to find our way home. Our sense of exile is a kind of living death, the death which the man and the woman were warned would issue from their desire to assert themselves over and against God. As the biblical story unfolds, it becomes clear that in order to come home, the attitude of the man and the woman demonstrated in the Fall, and which is in fact universal, has to be reversed. In order to find ourselves once again, we have to lose ourselves; in order truly to live, our separate selves have to die (Matthew 10.39, Mark 8.35, Luke 9.24, John 12.25). The whole biblical narrative is orientated towards the revelation that Jesus himself is the paradigm of this.

And yet there is, perhaps, a further subtlety in all this. As was mentioned earlier, there is a kind of dramatic irony in relation to the fact that the man and the woman do not yet know that they are like God. This raises the question as to how they would indeed come to know that for themselves. The obvious answer lies in exactly what does happen: through falling into duality. Duality brings with it the birth of self-consciousness and self-reflection of a certain kind, as well as the awareness that we are not at home with ourselves. It is this sense of things not quite being as they should be that actually precipitates the search for our true home. This is why the experience of suffering has the capacity to awaken us.

The mystery, therefore, is that the very thing which leads us into exile is the same thing that awakens in us the longing for home – for God and for our true self – and indeed propels us into the journey home. It is for this reason that the Fall itself is understood to be necessary in some mysterious way. The *Exultet*, the ancient chant sung in many churches on Easter Eve in celebration of the resurrection, proclaims towards the end: 'O truly necessary sin of Adam, destroyed completely by the Death of Christ! O happy fault that earned for us so great, so glorious a Redeemer!'[4] And this reminds us, too, of the statement made by Mother Julian of Norwich in her *Revelations of Divine Love*: 'Sin is necessary [behovable]' (Julian of Norwich 1966, p.103).

The Christian story, then, articulates for us the universal sense of exile, the consciousness that things are not as they should be, the awareness that there is a general unsatisfactoriness about life and the way things are in the world. It identifies the cause of this sense of homelessness as originating in the desire of human beings to assert themselves by separating themselves from God, in whose very image and likeness they are created, and going it alone. While this separation is understood at one level to be disastrous, at another level it is perceived to be the very thing that has the capacity to awaken us to who we truly are. Our true home is not one of duality, division and separation but non-duality, harmony and union. Our journey back to this 'original' state is by way of learning to surrender our egocentricity, in short by being willing to die to ourselves. When we do this, we wake up to the fact that we have actually been at home all the while, but have failed to realise it.

As the biblical story develops beyond the early chapters of Genesis, we discover that the sense of exile comes to be lived out in a literal manner. The Israelites become enslaved in Egypt and much later, in the sixth century BCE, the

---

4   The *Exultet* is thought to originate from no later than the fourth century, although the earliest extant manuscript is the *Bobbio Missal*, found in Bobbio Abbey, northern Italy, in 1686.

Israelites find themselves displaced from their home country and exiled to Babylon following invasion. The longing for home and an end to suffering becomes a perennial cry. It gives rise to the hope that one day everything will be restored to its original state. This hope is seen to be fulfilled in Jesus, who calls us to follow him on a path that will lead us home. When he so calls us, two things are implicit. First, that the path is one that involves dying: for him, literally dying on a cross, and for us, dying to our sense of separation. Second, when we respond to his call to follow, it is not simply a response to someone totally different from who we are. In responding to him, we are at the same time awakening to who we truly are. The one who is the very image and likeness of God, the 'exact imprint of God's very being' (Hebrews 1.3), enables us to see in him who we are as those created in the image and likeness of God. We awaken to our true selves and know ourselves to be at home.

The search for enlightenment

In the context of Zen, the aspiration to raise the Bodhi Mind is exemplified supremely in the life of Siddhārtha Gautama, who, ever since he experienced his own enlightenment in what is traditionally thought to have been 528 BCE, has been referred to simply as 'the Buddha', the 'Awakened One'.[5] As far as the details of the Buddha's life are concerned, there is a complex variety of sources. In many ways, this is a not

---

5   Armstrong notes that some scholars have argued for a later date in the
     first half of the fifth century (Armstrong 2000, p.73). Debates continue
     about the Buddha's actual dates, with the 'year of his death now being
     set anywhere between 486 and 360 BCE' (Strong 2001, p.1). Gombrich
     (2009, p.xiii) suggests that he 'must have died around 415'.

entirely dissimilar situation to that concerning the historical Jesus. After the death and resurrection of Jesus, numerous stories circulated about him and there were more gospels around at the time than the ones which eventually found their way into the New Testament. Gradually, though, decisions were made about what was to be included in canonical texts, as a result of which we now have the Bible as what has been deemed to be the definitive authority, even though other texts not included in the Bible are still available to read and consult.

It took time after the Buddha's death for biographical traditions to develop, but three 'layers' of tradition are discernible. First, there are biographical fragments in canonical texts, composed on the whole in Pali or Sanskrit. The second layer is that of 'fuller, more autonomous lives of the Buddha', of which some 'may have been incorporated into the Buddhist canon, or into commentaries on canonical texts, but, in all cases, they also enjoyed separate existences as biographical compositions in their own right' (Strong 2001, p.6). Finally, there is a 'host of comparatively late lives of the Buddha, composed in Sri Lanka, Southeast Asia, Tibet and East Asia, sometimes in one of the so-called canonical languages (Sanskrit, Pali, Tibetan, Chinese) but often in local vernaculars, for example, Sinhalese, Burmese, Thai, Khmer, Mongolian, Korean, Japanese' (Strong 2001, p.6).

Historical accuracy about the Buddha's life is hard to determine without equivocation, and when we consider that many of the stories in the Pali scriptures, for example, have an 'allegorical or symbolic meaning' (Armstrong 2000, p.xxi), it might be thought impossible to be confident about anything in relation to the Buddha's biography.

This need not give too much cause for concern, though. While there is a place for establishing historical facts, we have come to realise that in relation to the historical Jesus, for example, we can be sure of much less than we used to think. The important point, however, is that Christians have modelled their lives on him for centuries, and it is 'as a paradigm' that the gospels present Jesus (Armstrong 2000, p.xix). Much the same can be said of the Buddha, too. The various biographies, stories and other material are really there for teaching purposes, to enable the Buddha's followers to model their lives on his or, more particularly, on his teaching – the Dharma – which his life embodies. What follows, therefore, is nothing more than an outline, the gist, as it were, of what can be found in the various sources, specifically with a view to their relevance to Zen.

The story of the Buddha's life

Siddhārtha Gautama was born into a royal family. His parents – Śuddhodana and Māyā – of the Śākya clan, were King and Queen of Kapilavastu. As such, of course, it was assumed that Gautama would one day inherit the throne of the kingdom. One tradition, for example, has it that he descended into his mother's womb in the form of a great six-tusked white elephant. Clearly this is not intended to be taken literally. The great white elephant was one of the emblems of the *cakravartin* king, an ideal universal ruler, who rules over the entire world with wisdom and benevolence. The purpose of the story, therefore, is to underline the Buddha's sovereignty, although the issue of whether his rule would be temporal or spiritual is attested in the story of the 32 signs of a great man. According to tradition, Gautama's father invited 100 diviners to inspect the newly born baby's body, to see if there were any auspicious signs which might give some indication as to the child's future career. It was concluded that if the boy were to stay at home, he would become a great king. If he chose to become a wandering mendicant, however, he would become supremely awakened, a Buddha.[6]

Shielded from reality

'Living in exile' is not a phrase that would naturally spring to mind to describe Gautama's early life. Certainly, he lacked nothing in the eyes of the world; indeed, at a superficial level he had everything that many people long for. Material riches and security were his from the outset. Yet it is not difficult to detect the tell-tale signs of dissatisfaction sown early on in his life. Of overwhelming significance is the fact that his mother died when he was just a few days old.[7] By way of compensation, Gautama's father ensured that he was given all the attention he needed, and luxury after luxury was lavished on him. While a baby of a few days old can scarcely have had any knowledge of his mother's death at the time, it is not difficult to imagine that the impact of the loss would have been felt over time in the unconscious at the very least. In this sense, it would seem highly likely that the over-compensation made by his father for Gautama's mother's death, in the shape of all the luxury that the world

---

6   For further details, especially for a description of the 32 marks themselves, see Strong (2001, pp.54–58).

7   For an illuminating exploration of the impact of this event on the Buddha's life, see Epstein (2013a).

can afford, must have contributed over the course of time to a gnawing feeling that something was missing in Gautama's life. Put simply, the loss of his mother at an early age must have had a devastating impact on the young Gautama. This would have made itself felt only gradually, but it does not require much imagination to appreciate that although Gautama might not have been able to identify precisely what it was that was awry, the barely remembered loss of his mother would have contributed to the feeling that the life of luxury he was living was shallow and something of a distraction from the sense of dis-ease which hovered in the deeper recesses of his mind.

Although he would indeed leave his royal home at around the age of 29 – so it is generally thought – having glimpsed and been unsettled by something of the suffering of the world from which his father had sought to protect him, the feeling of dissatisfaction which prompted him to 'go forth' in search of enlightenment must surely have been fed to some extent by his early childhood loss. It would not seem to be overstating the case to say that the seeds of his awareness of suffering, which was the cause of his taking up the search in the first place, were sown just days after his birth. After his enlightenment, he would assert in the First Noble Truth that life is *duḥkha* or suffering. His incipient awareness of this truth was present, though obscured, from the start.

The 'First Meditation'

Over the course of time, other experiences would intensify Gautama's feeling of dissatisfaction. Little by little, he became disenchanted with his life. What is known as the

Buddha's 'First Meditation' took place when he went out to watch his father and the rest of the royal court take part in the festival marking the first ploughing of the fields. While sitting under a rose-apple tree, Gautama entered into something of a trance. When his father and others came to look for him, they noticed that while the shadows of all the other trees had moved, the tree under which Gautama was sitting was still in the shade, something which caused the King to bow in homage before him. While this meditative state enabled him to discover a sense of joy and peace deep within him, it also gave rise to an awareness of suffering. The sight of labouring oxen, sweating men and other insects and worms being turned over by the ploughs was perceived by Gautama to be a sign of the suffering which affects every aspect of life. Thus 'in a Chinese biography, a whole chain of suffering is narrated: the worms uncovered by the plough are snapped up by a frog, which is then swallowed by a snake, which is eaten by a peacock, which is killed by a hawk, which, in turn is devoured by an eagle' (Strong 2001, p.62). Of significance for the destiny of the Buddha-to-be, though, as Strong observes, is that this suffering is caused by a ploughing festival intended to reassert the sovereignty of the king. What entails suffering in this instance is the re-establishment of kingship. It is not entirely surprising, therefore, that Gautama was already turning in a different direction from inheriting the royal throne.

The 'Four Sights'

The other significant event, which has come to be referred to as the 'Four Sights' or 'Four Signs', has already been mentioned in passing above. The details in the accounts vary. Suffice to say, though, that Gautama is said to have encountered an old man while out for a ride in the pleasure park of the palace. Never having seen an old man before, Gautama was disconcerted, and asked his charioteer to explain why the man was in such a condition. The explanation given was that the man was simply old and that everyone who lived long enough would experience a similar decline. Whether on the same occasion or others, Gautama caught sight of a sick man, a corpse and a monk. The sight of the first two intensified Gautama's distress, but the third gave him hope that there was a way out of suffering. While he came to realise that old age, sickness and death were universal, the sight of the mendicant, who seemed to be at ease with himself and the world, suggested a way of coming to understand the nature of suffering. It was this that made him resolve to leave the environs of the palace in search of enlightenment.

Gautama decides to 'go forth'

Despite being married with a young son, the growing dissatisfaction with life that Gautama was feeling gave rise to bigger questions, questions that simply would not go away. It would be unwise to assume that the decision to 'go forth' was straightforward, though. Gautama experienced all sorts of inner conflicts about leaving home. Māra, 'a high-ranking god, one of the chief divinities of the realm of desire, and so a Lord of death and rebirth' (Strong 2001, p.92), 'the Lord of this world, the god of sin, greed and death' (Armstrong 2000, p.31), came to dissuade him from his chosen path by suggesting that he could do so much good as a benevolent ruler, and that he could end suffering as a result of benevolent government. Although Gautama held to his decision, Māra promised to be with him every step of the way. Armstrong suggests that Māra 'really represents what Jungian psychologists would, perhaps, call his shadow-side, all the unconscious elements in the psyche which fight against our liberation' (Armstrong 2000, p.32). It will be noted, no doubt, that there is a clear parallel here with the figure of the devil, who tempted Jesus in the wilderness after his baptism, and who, after Jesus resisted the temptations, 'departed from him until an opportune time' (Luke 4.13).

On leaving the palace, the first thing Gautama did after his Great Departure was to 'take off his princely jewels, to cut his hair with his own sword, and then to exchange his princely clothes for the robes of a monk' (Strong 2001, p.79). Thus began a six-year journey, during which Gautama would pursue a relentless search for the cause of his dissatisfaction with life, in the hope of putting an end to his restlessness, and of finding the peace of mind which had hitherto eluded him. If his departure from home seems dramatic, then it is worth saying that it was not as unusual then as we might now be inclined to think. To suggest that this sort of thing was something of a craze would be to trivialise the very serious intent with which many people engaged in a spiritual search at the time. Gautama was not alone, though, as he began his journey; there were many like him. And there was a whole variety of possibilities on offer to help him find what he was looking for.

Ignorance and desire

Broadly speaking, though, two factors were considered to be of paramount importance in hindering the path to spiritual liberation: ignorance and desire, and various schools, groups or *sanghas* gathered around this leader or that, who emphasised the one or the other. Those who argued that ignorance was the primary problem suggested that our suffering was the result of our failure to understand the nature of the true self, which was 'eternal and identical with the Absolute Spirit (*puruṣa*) that is dormant in every thing and every body but concealed by the material world of nature (*praktṛi*)' (Armstrong 2000, pp.40–41). The task for the seeker was to rise above the complex of emotions experienced within by attending to the purest part of the human being – the intellect – which has the capacity to reflect the eternal spirit. Once the aspirant became aware that his 'true self was entirely free, absolute and eternal' (Armstrong 2000, p.40), liberation would be attained, as a consequence of which the seeker could no longer be touched by suffering.

Those who advocated for desire as the chief cause of suffering were aware of the besetting problem of egotism. Every action is driven by desire in one way or another. Unless that were so, it is hard to conceive how anything would ever happen at all. Desire, after all, was the motivation for Gautama's embarking on a spiritual search in the first place. In this sense, desire is what lies behind the notion of *karma*, which basically means action, but which leads to consequences. All our actions are conditioned by our own previous actions and by those of others. Things go wrong, though, when desire is distorted and everything is focused on a grasping 'I', 'me', and 'mine', the lens through which we view the world and weigh up what the consequences of an action might be for 'me'. Suffering is the result of the human propensity to look after its own narrow interests at the expense of others. The eradication of desire, so it was assumed, therefore, was what would give access to the true self and bring about an end to suffering.

On his path towards enlightenment, Gautama would conclude that the diagnosis of both ignorance and desire as presenting barriers to its attainment rang true – and he found elements of practices designed to remove them helpful, especially yoga – but not completely so. Acting to extinguish desire often served only to intensify it, as anyone knows if they are deprived of such basic necessities as food, drink or warmth, to say nothing of love, affection and security. The more keenly their absence is felt, the more the desire for them is stoked. Ascetic practices, intended to bring the body and mind to heel, left Gautama feeling exhausted and ill, and no nearer the enlightenment he so desired. Similarly, although he appreciated the part played by ignorance as impeding his progress, he found the metaphysical doctrines that underpinned the various practices to remove it unsatisfactory. What he wanted was a direct and immediate experience of the unconditioned and uncreated self. Thought itself, along with passions, desires and other things over which he had no control, however, always intruded, creating a kind of internal distance and separation within himself. So it was that after nearly six years, he seemed to find himself as far from the end of his search as when he began.

The 'First Meditation' revisited

A potential solution suggested itself as the memory of his childhood meditation under the rose-apple tree began to surface in his mind. Recalling that the sense of joy, peace and compassion for suffering beings that he had experienced had arisen within him unbidden, he began to wonder whether what he was so desperately looking for was not in some way already present to him as part of his very nature. As a boy, he had experienced 'a moment of spiritual release' as a result of 'a surge of selfless empathy' for fellow suffering creatures (Armstrong 2000, p.61). He had in a sense been taken out of himself in a way that had nothing to do with craving and greed. Rather than make an assault on human nature, then, why not cultivate positive tendencies that sought to 'release the mind' (Armstrong 2000, p.61)?

His yogic training had included a significant ethical component. Prohibitions against killing, lying, stealing, taking intoxicants and engaging in sexual activities were intended to help reduce and eliminate the scope of egotistical desires. While killing, lying and stealing could rightly be seen as causing harm to others, and the use of intoxicants as dulling and impairing one's mental faculties, what – we might well ask from our twenty-first-century perspective – is wrong in principle with sexual activity? The answer surely lies in the fact that sex can be misused and motivated by pure egotism alone, by the unbridled desire for self-gratification. That is not the whole story, though. As an expression of love, sex can also be a beautiful thing. From the perspective of the doctrine widely held among the various yogis of the time, however, the belief that the Absolute Spirit was hidden in nature and somehow obscured by it required that nature – which included sex almost by definition – had to be transcended and left behind. Now although Gautama's musings were not prompted by thoughts about sex specifically, the foregoing remarks can help to give us a sense, perhaps, of how his mind worked. The total denial of sex goes against nature. Species, after all, would become extinct without procreation. However, engaging in sexual activity purely for self-gratification is to debase both sex itself and one's sexual partner. A middle way between the two is what is required.

It was precisely such a middle way that presented itself to Gautama as the solution he was looking for. Rather than try to control himself by ways which seemed to be an assault against his very humanity, why not cultivate those very natural and spontaneous attitudes he had experienced in his boyhood meditation? So it was that Gautama began to practise the positive virtues of 'love, compassion, empathetic joy and equanimity' and after his enlightenment 'declared them to be direct routes to nirvana, the supreme bliss' (Gombrich 2009, p.90).

At the risk of getting slightly ahead of ourselves here, it is worth making a slight digression at this juncture to draw attention to the fact that the Five Precepts, which are the same prohibitions as those already referred to above, are still binding on all Buddhists today. These are expressed negatively as not taking the life of any living being, not taking what is not given, abstaining from sexual misconduct, abstaining from wrong speech and abstaining from intoxicants. In Zen, particularly, however, they are expressed both positively and negatively. 'Do not kill' is thus expressed as 'affirm life'; 'do not steal' as 'be giving'; 'do not misuse sexuality' as 'honour the body'; 'do not lie' as 'manifest truth'; and 'do not misuse intoxicants' as 'proceed clearly – do not cloud the mind' (Loori 1996, pp.84, 88, 89, 91, 93). The correspondence between four of the above precepts and four of the Ten Commandments

(Exodus 20.1–17; Deuteronomy 5.6–21) will surely not go unnoticed. It is interesting to note, however, that of the Ten Commandments, all but two are expressed negatively, the exceptions being the fourth and the fifth: 'Observe the Sabbath day and keep it holy' and 'Honour your father and mother'. Perhaps it is the feel of the negative prohibition which gives us an insight into what Gautama was after. While it is our experience that excesses do indeed need to be reined in from time to time, the danger is that without discernment, an overemphasis on prohibitions runs the risk of doing violence to our own nature. The cultivation of positive attitudes, by contrast, allows our own self-nature to manifest itself quite freely and naturally because we are able to realise the way things 'really are', no longer needing to struggle 'against [our] deepest grain' (Armstrong 2000, p.75). Nirvana is to be found within us, if we are prepared to let it manifest itself.

Recalling his meditation under the rose-apple tree, tradition has it that Gautama sat down under a Bodhi tree and resolved not to get up until he had found what he was looking for. Thus he sat and meditated all night long. What, it might well be asked, did he experience that night? What was the nature of the enlightenment he claimed to have realised? The essence of his experience was eventually formulated in what are now known as the Four Noble Truths. Put simply they are these: Life is suffering; the cause of suffering is craving; it is possible for suffering to cease; the way to the cessation of suffering is by following the Eightfold Noble Path. This path embraced morality (*sila*): right speech, right action and right livelihood; meditation (*samādhi*): right effort, right mindfulness and right concentration; and wisdom (*pannā*): right understanding and right resolve. Armstrong (2000, p.74) observes that there 'seems nothing strikingly original about these truths' and that 'most of the monks and ascetics of North India would have agreed with the first three'. Indeed, Gautama himself had 'been convinced of them since the very beginning of his quest'. Whatever was new had to do with the fourth truth, the 'way he had found to enlightenment, a method which he called the Noble Eightfold Path'. Armstrong's insight into what actually occurred on that auspicious night is worth quoting at length:

> If there is any truth to the story that Gotama gained enlightenment at Bodh Gayā in a single night, it could be that he acquired a sudden, absolute certainty that he really *had* discovered a method that would, if followed energetically, bring an earnest seeker to Nibbāna. He had not made this up; it was not a new creation or an invention of his own. On the contrary, he had always insisted that he simply discovered 'a path of great antiquity, an ancient trail, travelled by human beings in a far-off, distant era'. The other Buddhas, his predecessors, had taught this path an immeasurably long time ago, but this ancient knowledge had faded over the years and had been entirely forgotten. Gotama insisted that this insight was simply a statement of things 'as they really are'; the path was written into the very structure of existence. It was, therefore, the Dhamma, par excellence, because it elucidated the fundamental principles of existence. If men, women, animals and gods kept to this path, they could all attain enlightenment that would bring them peace and fulfilment, because they were no longer struggling against their deepest grain. (Armstrong 2000, p.75)

What seems to have happened as he sat under the Bodhi tree is that these truths, which are capable of making rational sense, did not come to him by means of discursive reasoning. Rather, it was by letting go of all egotism that these truths emerged from within, beyond the workings of rational understanding. So absorbed was he in these truths, with nothing coming between them and him, that he apprehended them directly. In so doing, he, like anyone who seeks enlightenment, was 'in tune with the fundamental structure of the universe' (Armstrong 2000, p.84). Being in tune, in harmony, with everything that exists in this way, gave rise to the realisation that there is no separation, no duality. Zen tradition has it that Gautama realised enlightenment when he caught sight of the morning star as he sat meditating under the Bodhi tree that night. The heart of his experience is thus encapsulated in the following *kōan*: 'Shakyamuni Buddha saw the morning star and was enlightened and said, "I and the great earth and beings simultaneously achieve the Way"' (Cook 2003, p.29).

Summary: a mutual sense of exile

This chapter has sought to show that Christianity and Zen are at one in their recognition that we are not at home in one way or another, that our experience of life is characterised by a mysterious sense of exile and alienation. The biblical story of the Fall, together with Jesus' parable of the Prodigal Son, beautifully convey an awareness that the cause of our alienation lies in our grasping at what we think we desire and need, all the while failing to recognise that what we are grasping for is already ours in the first place.

The story of the Buddha's search for enlightenment, for all that it is not possible to be unequivocally certain about the detailed historical facts of his life, provides, nevertheless, a paradigm of the universal search for our spiritual home. Despite the privileged circumstances of his birth, he became aware of a gnawing sense of dissatisfaction, which was intensified when he came across concrete suffering for the first time, and which was only alleviated when he discovered that the answer to what he was looking for was already present in himself as his own true nature, a nature characterised by selfless empathy, compassion, love and joy. The realisation of his true nature was at one and the same time the awakening to the original state of non-duality.

While non-duality is not in itself a Christian term, the story of the Fall in the book of Genesis discloses our original state, nevertheless, to be one of harmony, in which there is no separation – although there is distinctiveness – or division. When we identify separation as the ultimate state, we are in fact deluded. In both Zen and Christianity, our sense of exile arises from the grasping of the ego, which sees everything as separate and isolated, and which refers everything to its own narrow and limited self-interest. It is this misguided perception that Christianity and Zen, in their different and distinctive ways, both seek to deal with.

Chapter 2

Finding the Way Home

Coming home to ourselves

In the previous chapter, I suggested that there is something in our experience that gives us the sense that we are living in exile, that we are not at home with ourselves, with others, with the created order, with God. The universal experience of suffering is what gives rise in no small way to this awareness of dis-ease. In the Christian tradition, this is encapsulated in Jesus' parable known as the Prodigal Son, which in many ways can be seen as a distillation of the whole biblical story. In the first three chapters of Genesis, which include the myths of the Creation and the Fall, the human condition is diagnosed in a remarkably evocative and succinct way.

Just as the biblical narrative evokes the journey from exile to homecoming, so in Buddhism it is the story of the Buddha's life itself which traces this trajectory. From the privileged circumstances into which he was born, to his first encounters with old age, sickness, death and holiness, his departure from home, his search for enlightenment, and his awakening as he sat under the Bodhi tree, his story is presented as a universal paradigm for human beings to find a way out of exile and discover their true home. In this context, the goal of the human search might be characterised as coming home to ourselves and, in so doing, coming home to everything, a state in which there is no separation and no division. It is not insignificant that the Buddha's realisation occurred when he finally stopped moving and sat down under the tree to meditate. While Zen is concerned with every aspect of life, the practice of seated meditation – *zazen* – is at its heart. *Zazen* is at one and the same time both the path to realisation and the very manifestation of it.

What I should like to do in this chapter, then, is to explore exactly how the practice of Zen serves to wake us up to our home and provides what at this stage can only be described as a pathless path to that home. Zen abounds in paradox, and 'pathless path' is just one such, the reasons for which I hope will be sensed, as it were, rather than worked out rationally, as the book proceeds. Using the story of Bodhidharma (c.440–c.530 CE), I hope to be able to give a flavour of what is involved in practising Zen in the form of both *zazen* and *kōan* study as a way of discovering home. I shall then relate this to the Christian tradition, especially as found in some of the teachings of Jesus, showing that what is labelled 'Zen' can also be seen in Jesus' approach.

So, let us plunge straight in with a *kōan* about Bodhidharma. All that needs to be known at this initial stage is that the word '*kōan*' simply means 'public case' and is more often than not simply the story, account or anecdote of a fairly brief exchange between a Zen master and a student or between two Zen masters. *Kōans* are to be found in a variety of collections, of which there are primarily four, each compiled by one Zen master or another.[1] As they appear in the collections, there are usually three parts to the *kōan*: the case (i.e. the story) itself, a commentary by the compiler of the collection and, finally a verse, usually referred to as the 'capping verse'. The following *kōan* is Case 41 in *The Gateless Gate*, a collection put together by Mumon Ekei (1183–1260) and known as the *Mumonkan*.[2]

Bodhidharma Puts the Mind to Rest

The case

Bodhidharma sat facing the wall. The second patriarch, standing in the snow, cut off his arm and said, 'Your disciple's mind is not yet at peace. I beg you, Master, give it rest.'

Bodhidharma said, 'Bring your mind to me and I will put it to rest.'

The patriarch said, 'I have searched for the mind but have never been able to find it.'

---

1   These are *The Blue Cliff Record* (*Hekiganroku*), *The Book of Equanimity* (*Shōyōroku*) *The Gateless Gate* or *The Gateless Barrier* (*Mumonkan*) and *The Record of Transmitting the Light* (*Denkōroku*). In some cases, the same individual *kōan* is to be found in more than one than collection.

2   Many *kōan* collections today appear with additional commentaries by more contemporary Zen masters. For the text of the *kōans* in *The Gateless Gate* without such a commentary, see Mumon (2006). For collections with commentaries by modern Zen masters, see especially Shibayama (2000) and Yamada (2004). This particular *kōan* is to be found in Mumon (2006, p.81), Shibayama (2000, pp.285–292) and Yamada (2004, pp.194–198).

Bodhidharma said, 'I have finished putting it to rest for you.'

Mumon's commentary

The broken-toothed old barbarian came thousands of miles across the sea with an active spirit. It can rightly be said that he raised waves where there was no wind. In later life he obtained one disciple, but even he was crippled in his six senses. Ha! The fools do not even know four characters.

The verse

Coming from the west and pointing directly to it –
All the trouble comes from the transmission;
The one who disturbs the monasteries
Is originally you.

Penetrating the *kōan*

To anyone who has not encountered a *kōan* before, this is likely to be deeply perplexing, but that is most definitely not something to be worried about. Indeed, it is to be welcomed, embraced and accepted. Its very strangeness is largely the point in the first instance. Being somewhat at sea with a *kōan* is the way a *kōan* calls into question our habitual ways of seeing, understanding and apprehending. If we stay with a *kōan* long enough, it is almost certain to make us feel uncomfortable, stupid and ignorant. It is in this place that we are most open to what the *kōan* is getting at.

So, why not reread the *kōan* above – slowly – and resist the temptation to fight against the ways in which we have been encouraged to believe that what matters is that we are in control and that knowledge is power, and consider for just one outrageous moment that it might be the other way round, that *not knowing* might be the clue to what we are really looking for and is what will bring us peace of mind. As you read it again, pause over words and phrases that disconcert you and stay with that feeling of discomfort. My hunch is that certain phrases will almost certainly cause irritation and frustration. Why, you might ask, was Bodhidharma facing a wall? Why did the second patriarch commit an act of horrendous self-mutilation by cutting off his arm, and is that the kind of thing that is involved in Zen practice and what Zen commends? What about the mind? Do we not know exactly what the mind is? So why was the second patriarch unable to find it? What did Bodhidharma do to put to rest a mind that cannot be found?

Similar questions will be prompted by the commentary and verse. Who is the broken-toothed barbarian? If, as may reasonably be assumed, it is Bodhidharma himself, then why is he described in this way? Is it intended as a term of abuse? In what way did he raise waves where there was no wind? And who is the disciple? Is it the second patriarch – Huike – and what does it mean to suggest that he was crippled in his six senses, and that the fools – whoever they are – do not know four characters? The verse raises questions in the same vein. What is the 'it' that is pointed to in the first line and what does it mean to point to 'it'? What is the 'transmission' and what does it have to do with monasteries? And finally, in what way are you or I – the ones addressed in the last line – the one who disturbs the monasteries?

Some of our reactions might well lead us to conclude that this *kōan* inhabits a world of nonsense. If we are to allow the *kōan* to yield its secrets, though, we have not to fight shy of our inclination to run away and give up on it as something of a bad job, and instead just let it do its work on us as we push it and probe it, often to no avail. *Kōans* are not irrational but they do open up for us a realm that transcends what we ordinarily think of as rationality. They invite us to see things differently. Not everything about a *kōan* is opaque, though. Certain information is needed to enable us to appreciate some of the actual text itself on the surface level, so let us start with a little background.

Background to the *kōan*

The historical significance of Bodhidharma lies in the fact that it was he who 'brought' Zen from India – the 'West' referred to in the verse – to China in the fifth century, as a result of which, though actually being Indian, he is known as the first Chinese Zen Patriarch. The notion of 'bringing' Zen, though, immediately brings to light the inherently paradoxical nature of Zen – in the same way that 'pathless path' does. There is actually nothing to be 'brought', for 'it' – the 'it' at the end of the first line of the verse – is already 'there'. There is nothing to be attained, nothing to be gained that we do not already have. Rather 'it' is 'there', waiting to be discovered, as Shakyamuni Buddha[3] found out himself as he sat under the Bodhi tree. It is about awakening rather than getting. The following verse,

---

3   'Shakyamuni' is an honorific of the historical Buddha, meaning 'Sage of the Shakyas', deriving from Śākya, the name of the clan into which he was born.

attributed to Bodhidharma, seeks to convey something of what the Zen way is:

> A special transmission outside the scriptures,
> Not founded upon words and letters;
> By pointing directly to [one's] the mind
> It lets one see into [one's own true] nature, and [thus] attain Buddhahood. (Dumoulin 2005a, p.85)[4]

Whatever is it that is being transmitted, then? Do not run away from that question; just stay with it, for this question begins to take us to a deeper level of the *kōan*, the 'answer' to which can only be discovered for ourselves; it cannot be apprehended second-hand. The intention of the *kōan* is to enable us to awaken to this 'it', and such awakening cannot be forced; we simply have to wait for it patiently. Information relating to the superficial level of the text can clear the ground a little, though, and begin to help us to discern what the *kōan* is getting at, so let us continue with some more of the background.

Bodhidharma was the third son of a king in southern India. On one occasion when Bodhidharma was young and still under the tutelage of the king's teacher, Hannyatara, he was shown a precious jewel. Bodhidharma reacted by saying that compared with the Dharma-treasure it was nothing, for the Dharma-treasure alone is supreme. Even as a boy, then, Bodhidharma demonstrated a rather heightened and acute spiritual sensitivity. After the death of his father, Bodhidharma continued to be a disciple of

---

4 'This verse is first found as a fixed formula in the *Sōtei join* (Chin., Tsu-t'ing *shih-yüan*), dating from 1108' (Dumoulin 2005a, p.102, n.1).

Hannyatara for 40 years, but as the venerable master was dying, he expressed the wish that Bodhidharma should go to China 60 years after his master's death. The arithmetic implies that Bodhidharma was getting on for 120 years old when he made an arduous three-year journey by boat to China in fulfilment of his teacher's dying wish.[5]

On his arrival in China, Bodhidharma's reputation as an awakened master seems to have preceded him, and he was summoned into the presence of Emperor Wu (502–549 CE) – a devout Buddhist himself, much given to the study of texts, who both wrote commentaries and also built and refurbished numerous Buddhist temples – who was keen to meet him and, so it would appear, discuss various doctrinal matters with him. Among these was the question of whether all his efforts in relation to Buddhism were of any advantage to him.

Thus it was that when Emperor Wu first met Bodhidharma, he asked him what merit he would have acquired on account of his various activities. 'No merit whatsoever', was Bodhidharma's response. The Emperor had clearly been expecting the conventional answer that

---

5 Zen masters are often said to have lived to a considerable age in much the same way that the biblical patriarchs are said to have done. Abraham, for example, is recorded as having been 175 years old when he died (Genesis 25.7) and Joseph 110 (Genesis 50.26). Zen Master Jōshu – Chinese: Zhaozhou – (778–897 CE) was apparently 120 when he died (Ferguson 2011, p.153). Ferguson (2011) provides excellent, scholarly and well-researched information about the Chinese Zen masters from the first to the twenty-fifth generations, beginning with Bodhidharma and ending with Wumen Huikai (1183–1260), known in Japanese as Mumon, as does Dumoulin (2005a). For a less academic but very readable introduction, covering not just the Chinese heritage of Zen but its worldwide development, and extending to the present day, see Ford (2006).

he had accrued considerable merit, so it is not surprising that he was rather taken aback. Indeed, he might even have thought that Bodhidharma was not actually the real thing, perhaps not even the real person he had heard about, but something of an imposter. This seems to be why the Emperor then asked Bodhidharma who it was who was facing Wu himself. 'I don't know', came the reply (Ferguson 2011, p.15; Cleary & Clearly 2013, p.1). Sensing that there was no point in pursuing the conversation, Bodhidharma turned on his heels and left the south of China and ventured towards the north, where he sat and faced a wall – in other words, he sat *zazen*, seated meditation – for nine years.

Back to the *kōan*

It is while Bodhidharma was thus sitting that the incident at the heart of the *kōan* occurred. The second patriarch, referred to in the *kōan* is Huike, about whom there seem to be two traditions. One suggests that as a boy Huike had developed a love of reading, and while poring over a Buddhist text on one occasion had a great insight, which inspired him to become a monk. As such, he devoted himself to further study and became a man of great learning (Shibayama 2000, p.286). According to the other, Huike had been a ruthless general and had won many battles, but the more he killed, the more unsettled and disturbed he became. On happening upon some Buddhist teachings, he felt contrition and resolved to become a monk. He spent his time chanting the *sūtras* and wandering from teacher to teacher, but still could not find the peace of mind he longed for (Gu 2016, p.336). It is in desperation, so it would seem, that he approached Bodhidharma, possibly as a last resort, or simply because he sensed for the first time in his life, perhaps, that here was the one person who could help him at last.

Bodhidharma's initial response was to dismiss Huike: 'I have nothing to give you, nothing to teach; go away.' Snow was falling outside where Huike was patiently standing and persistently waiting, and the story goes that he remained there until he was knee-deep in snow. Huike was not going to take no for an answer. Clearly, he must have intuited that Bodhidharma had exactly what he himself was looking for. What was it about sitting and facing a wall for nine years that led him to believe that his search ended here or nowhere? In order to impress on Bodhidharma his utter seriousness of intent, he drew his sword, cut off his arm, presented it to Bodhidharma and said: 'Your disciple's mind is not yet at peace. I beg you, Master, give it rest.'

In order to appreciate just what is going on here, let us pause for a moment to reflect. If we were to describe Huike's condition, it would surely not be overstating the case to suggest that he was in agony in every way. Put simply, he was suffering, and nothing ever relieved his pain and anguish. The fact that he might have been a monk from an early age, or a ruthless general who later became a monk, is actually neither here nor there. In fact, it rather helps that he might have been both, for either throws light on the fact that our pain is ultimately a dis-ease of the mind. If Huike had been a general, the implication would be that he was troubled by guilt and remorse on account of the brutality with which he had caused the suffering and death of countless people. However much he tried, he just could not get rid of what troubled him. However, whether as a monk from a young age or as a monk following a military career, the study of doctrinal matters had also failed to satisfy him, but rather created a state of agitation. Even if a doctrine might point us in the right direction, it is not the reality itself, in the same way that a recipe book is not the food. It is an idea, a thought, a concept. To assume that the words and concepts through which a doctrine itself is articulated are in some sense identical with the reality they seek to evoke only serves to create a certain distance between us and that to which the doctrine points. Excessive concentration on and identification with the abstract formulation of a doctrine in the end separates us from the reality and leads to a deep sense of alienation. As is always the case, however, the *kōan*, as these reflections are probably already beginning to indicate, is not only about Huike, it is about you and me. Right now, at this moment, you and I are Huike and this *kōan* is about your life and mine. So how does it relate to your life?

Peace of mind is something we all long for. We fret about all sorts of things, some trivial and some serious. At this very moment, you might be in the kind of pain and anguish that Huike experienced. Perhaps you are tormented by guilt, or struggling to find any meaning or purpose in your life, or longing for a loving and fulfilling relationship, or searching for something to make sense of life intellectually. Alternatively, you might be able to recall a period in the past when you were in utter turmoil, searching in vain for relief. In such instances, we seem to be driven to distraction – sometimes literally, as we look for all sorts of things to take the pain away. As was mentioned in the previous chapter, we can resort to anything from using intoxicants to working too hard as a way of numbing the pain. It is as if we want to get away from ourselves. Pain of whatever kind consumes us, and we seem to become wholly identified with it. It colours our experience of everything, the whole of life, and we seem to be reduced by it. Life contracts and so do we; we become closed in on ourselves. At our lowest ebb, we might even find ourselves thinking: 'I'd give my right arm to be free of this pain. Anything would be better than this'.[6] In some cases, of course, it can be even worse: we simply long for oblivion and might even consider ending it all.

If this is how life is for you at the moment, or if you have experienced something like this at some other stage in your life, you are completely at one with Huike. Whether he literally cut off his arm or not, Huike had been brought to a point in his life where finding a cure for his pain, discovering how his mind could be put at rest, was the supremely burning issue for him. Nothing else mattered as much as this, and in trying to resolve this matter he had presumably done everything, from studying and trying to 'crack' various doctrines, to changing his lifestyle. Yet he was still disturbed: 'Your disciple's mind is not yet at peace. I beg you, Master, give it rest.' It was as if all his energy was concentrated into this longing for peace. He must have been like a coiled spring or a pressure cooker, in whom the tension was at breaking or exploding point.

---

6   Perhaps something of this lies behind Jesus' teaching, when he says: 'If your hand or foot causes you to stumble, cut it off and throw it away; it is better for you to enter life maimed or lame than to have two hands or feet and to be thrown into eternal fire. And if your eye causes you to stumble, tear it out and throw it away; it is better for you to enter life with one eye than to have two and to be thrown into the hell of fire' (Matthew 18.8–9).

Huike was, perhaps, rather taken aback by Bodhidharma's response to his request to give him peace of mind. Although the exchange between them suggests that Huike's realisation was immediate, it could just as easily have been gradual. Did Huike, for example, go away for a while and engage in prolonged periods of meditation in search of his mind and then return to tell Bodhidharma that he simply could not find it? Or was Bodhidharma's instruction to Huike to bring his mind to him the very thing that uncoiled the spring or released the pressure? Either way, Huike clearly found the relief he was looking for. What was it? A little explanation of what happens when we sit *zazen* might be of help here.

Zazen and emptiness

It is often assumed that sitting *zazen* requires us to empty our minds and make them vacant. This is a virtual impossibility. Sitting *zazen* brings us face to face with ourselves and, in so doing, we become aware of just what is going on in our minds. Thoughts arise incessantly, and it would appear that for the most part we have little or no control over whether thoughts arise or not. If we come to *zazen* in the expectation that we will no longer be troubled by thoughts of any kind, we will almost certainly be disappointed and quickly come to the conclusion that we are useless at it and have no aptitude for it whatsoever. It is as if we can never get away from our thoughts. The problem is that we identify ourselves with our thoughts. In the West, in particular, we have unconsciously accepted the dictum of the French philosopher, René Descartes (1596–1650), 'I think, therefore I am' (Descartes [1637] in Cottingham, Stoothoff & Murdoch 1985, p.127), and so we conclude with him that we are nothing more than a 'thinking thing' (Descartes [1641] in Cottingham, Stoothoff & Murdoch 1984, pp.18–19).

As we sit *zazen*, we become aware of a certain irony. Whereas we assume from one point of view that our self is determined by what we think, we discover from another point of view that this self is something of a fantasy, and it is precisely the creation of this self that is the problem and the cause of our dis-ease and anguish. In a way, we 'create' ourselves with each thought that comes and goes, from one moment to the next. We have an idea – just that: an idea – of who we think we and others are, and we think that this self, this construct, is who we really are. Who we are, though, is much more than what we think, yet when we look for whatever this is as an objective entity, we cannot find it. It is as if we try to look for our eyes with our eyes, failing to appreciate that our eyes are the very means by which we see in the first place. It is this that gives rise to Zen's speaking of emptiness.

Emptiness is liable to considerable misunderstanding, especially when it is turned into another abstract concept, a 'thing'. Emptiness does not mean sheer vacancy, nor does it imply nihilism. When we experience the self as empty, we discover this emptiness to be the source of an infinitely dynamic energy, creativity and compassion. But we cannot see this emptiness objectively, for that would be to make it something separate from ourselves, whereas it is just what we are. Nor does this mean that we do not exist. There is an objective world, of course, but in that world, nothing is of itself an independent, substantial reality. Furthermore, life is characterised by transiency and impermanence. Things come and go, we are born and we die, and this is true of everything. Our inclination, however, is to cling to things, people, thoughts, ideas, sensations and emotions in the rather vain hope of trying to control things and gain some kind of security, but in so doing we actually impede the natural flow of life. We get fixated ourselves and things get stuck.

It is this that robs us of peace, so peace is restored, as it were, when we adopt an attitude of letting go, of releasing our grip on things. In the process, it becomes clear that identifying ourselves with our thoughts serves to restrict our sense of who we are. Letting them go enables us to realise that who we are is expansive, all-embracing and all-inclusive. We are separate from nothing, everything is profoundly interconnected and interrelated. Peace of mind is attained when we give up fighting and resisting what arises in the mind and in our lives and accept with an all-embracing compassion whatever is present. It is this compassionate acceptance that diminishes the grip that distressing thoughts, passions and emotions have on us. Little by little, we let go, the spring uncoils and our dis-ease begins to be replaced by peace. This deep peace is who we truly are, and it is born of emptiness, which is also what we truly are.

Back to Huike

It is something of this that Huike came to realise when he declared that he had searched for his mind but was unable to find it. When Bodhidharma asked him to bring his mind to him, he neither denied the mind nor the anguish that Huike felt, but with immense compassion accepted Huike for who he was. In so doing he 'pointed directly' to what Huike did not have to find anywhere other than in himself, as a result of which the 'transmission' of mind to mind occurred. And yet there is nothing to be transmitted! After all, 'it' is already 'there'!

Sitting *zazen* or allowing a *kōan* to work on us invariably reveals to us that it is what we hang on to that obscures who we really are. Zen is supremely about letting go and allowing our true self to manifest itself quite naturally. Our habitual state of mind is so often one in which we are vexed. It seems to be counter-intuitive to trust that it is simply by letting go of vexations that peace of mind is restored. It is simple but not always easy. We can spend a lifetime of not quite learning the lesson. When we do, though, the scales fall from our eyes and we begin to see things clearly. All our thoughts and vexations are seen for what they are: delusions distorting and skewing reality. And yet, paradoxically, delusions are not dealt with by pummelling them out of existence; that only gives them more power over us. As soon as we stop fighting them and accept them, they begin to relax their hold on us and cease to trouble us any longer, even if we continue to be aware of their presence.

Mumon's commentary and verse

The purpose of Mumon's commentary and verse is to focus and draw out the essence of the *kōan*, to point us towards its heart. In this case, they underline the fact that we have no need to attain anything outside ourselves, nor, indeed, could we if we tried – despite our never-ending attempts to do so – because we already are what we seek. Not surprisingly, it was this teaching that created difficulties for Bodhidharma when he first arrived in China. Not unlike

Huike, the monks in China spent much of their time discussing the *sūtras*, arguing this point of detail and that, advocating one interpretation over another. Bodhidharma's message was that the scriptures, helpful and necessary though they may be at one level, are, in the end 'fingers pointing to the moon'. So often we are mesmerised by the finger and miss the moon altogether. This is exactly the issue with which Jesus confronted his opponents in the Gospel of John: 'You search the scriptures because you think that in them you have eternal life; and it is they that testify on my behalf. Yet you refuse to come to me to have life' (John 5.39–40). Here is a classic case of missing the moon for the finger. Just as Jesus stirred up his opponents, so did Bodhidharma 'disturb the monasteries'.

So enraged were the Chinese monks by Bodhidharma's message that they tried to poison him. It seems that Bodhidharma put the poison to his mouth, but on tasting it refrained from consuming the rest. Some poison, however, touched his tooth, causing it to break, hence he is described as the 'broken-toothed old barbarian', which is not so much a term of contempt as a designation that he was from foreign parts. The commentary reminds us, though, of the great lengths to which Bodhidharma went – and the personal cost involved – in 'bringing' the Zen way to China. In this sense, Bodhidharma models one of the three conditions required for the practice of Zen, namely, great determination: 'The ancients spoke of three essential conditions for Zen practice: First: great faith; second: great doubt; third: great determination. These are like the three legs of a tripod' (Yamada 2015, p.170).[7]

---

7   This was touched on in passing in the Introduction.

Great faith means that we and 'all beings are intrinsically awake'(Yamada 2015, p.169). This is our true nature, except that we fail to see it. This was partly what Huike struggled with. He could perceive in Bodhidharma something that he longed for, but he could not find it within himself – until Bodhidharma asked him to bring his mind to him. Being unable to find it, he awoke, as it were, to his own already awakened state. Huike certainly seems to have had great doubt, although doubt in the Zen context is not simply intellectual doubt. Doubt certainly involves a sense that 'this is not it' and 'that is not it', but this has to do with the delusory identification of ourselves with thought, thus creating a 'separate' self, distanced from our own experience. Great doubt characterises what is involved in the dismissal of all concepts and the inability to rest contentedly with anything other than who we really are. In other words, great doubt is coterminous with letting go. Once again, Huike was at one with his great doubt: he was utterly absorbed in it. Great determination simply describes our total commitment to practise, to realise what others have also realised in the past. Great determination thus underpins the faith, however strong or weak it may be at times, that we are intrinsically awake. In cutting off his arm, whether literally or metaphorically, Huike undoubtedly demonstrated great determination, mirroring Bodhidharma's own determination in 'bringing' Zen to China.

We know little about the effect of Bodhidharma's influence on individuals in China, other than on Huike himself, except that Zen became established as a result of his presence and teaching. The purpose of Bodhidharma's journey from India to China, though, was not to bring something that was not there already. Zen invites us to discover that all beings are already awake. What Bodhidharma did was to enable people to see into their true nature as already awakened beings. This is why the commentary describes Bodhidharma's journey as having the effect of raising waves where there was no wind. From the perspective of emptiness, there is nothing to raise: we are already enlightened, awake. From the perspective of our everyday experience, though, the waves need to be stirred up, so that we might discover and wake up to our own truth.

There is little more that needs to be said about the commentary and the verse. The last two sentences of the commentary appear to be rather derisory and mocking: 'In later life he [Bodhidharma] obtained one disciple [Huike], but even he was crippled in his six senses. Ha! The fools do not even know four characters.' The style, however, is typically ironic, where verbal abuse actually intends to convey the opposite, in much the same way that in recent times the words 'wicked' and 'sick' in English usage have, in some quarters, been used to mean things like 'fantastic' and 'great'. Mumon is thus praising Bodhidharma and Huike. Being crippled in his six senses[8] points to emptiness. Neither Bodhidharma nor Huike knowing four characters implies illiteracy – not knowing – and thus points to emptiness in a similar way.

The verse highlights the fact that in coming to China, Bodhidharma 'brought' nothing with him but could only 'point' to what was there – to who we are – already.

---

8   The mind itself is regarded as the sixth sense in Zen, in addition to the five bodily senses

Such 'transmission' as there was – of what cannot be transmitted – from Bodhidharma to Huike, was none other than our own truth and the truth of all beings as we already are: 'The one who disturbs the monasteries is originally you.'

This exploration of *Bodhidharma Puts the Mind to Rest* has shown that this *kōan*, like any other, invites us to see things differently, to see into our true nature, to see who we really are. In so doing, it turns our world upside down. As we sit with this *kōan*, we wake up to what we already are, not by trying to grasp the matter but by letting go. As we are taken beyond our ordinary rational and dualistic way of thinking, we awaken to emptiness, interconnectedness, wisdom and compassion. Wisdom is precisely what arises as a result of seeing into our true nature and it is expressed in our lives supremely as compassion.

The teaching of Jesus

We now turn our attention to the Christian tradition and, in particular, to the teachings of Jesus. Whatever else might be said of Jesus, it can be fairly said, I think, that he, too, turns our world upside down. He stands our habitual ways of seeing ourselves, others, the world and God, on their heads. Epigrammatic sayings, such as, 'So the last will be first, and the first will be last' (Matthew 20.16), 'Whoever wishes to be great among you must be your servant and whoever wishes to be first among you must be your slave' (Matthew 21.26–27), and 'All who exalt themselves will be humbled, and all who humble themselves will be exalted' (Matthew 23.12), are obvious examples of just this kind of turning things upside down. The ultimate reversal, of course, is the cross itself, of which more will be said in Part 2 of this book.

For the purposes of this chapter, however, I should like to focus on the teaching of Jesus in what is known as the 'Sermon on the Mount' in the Gospel of Matthew and, especially, on the passage where Jesus refers to the birds of the air and the lilies of the field in order to say something about anxiety (Matthew 6.25–34). This will be followed by looking at the account in the Gospel of Mark of the meeting between Jesus and a man who asks him what he must do to inherit eternal life, to see how Jesus' response to being called 'Good Teacher' might illuminate what was said in connection with the *kōan* above about how we 'create' ourselves from moment to moment by our thinking (Mark 10.17–22). Finally, I shall explore one or two passages in the gospels where Jesus responds to his opponents' attempts to trap him, by showing how he deals with this by transcending their habitual approach of thinking dualistically – just the kind of thing Zen invites us to do, too. The significant point to note, however, is that in pondering these teachings, we are not to think of them in an objective manner, as being somehow external to ourselves. Just as a Zen *kōan* points to who we really are as being intrinsically awake already, so, in a not dissimilar way, do the teachings of Jesus. To use Zen terminology, we are to become one with them. In this sense, we respond to the apostle Paul's injunction to 'let the same mind be in you that was in Christ Jesus' (Philippians 2.5).

The Sermon on the Mount

Much of the Sermon on the Mount is about letting go of our customary ways of seeing and thinking. The sermon begins with what are known as the Beatitudes: 'Blessed are the poor in spirit, for theirs is the kingdom of heaven' (Matthew 5.3). It is actually Luke's version of the same words which is more striking and blunt: 'Blessed are you who are poor, for yours is the kingdom of God' (Luke 6.20).[9] The gospel proceeds to acclaim those who hunger and weep (6.21), as well as those who are hated, excluded, reviled and defamed (Luke 6.22), and then to deride those who are rich (Luke 6.24), satiated and laughing (Luke 6.25). Matthew, by contrast, 'spiritualises' the teaching, so that 'poor' becomes 'poor in spirit' (Matthew 5.3) and those who 'hunger' becomes those who 'hunger and thirst for righteousness' (Matthew 5.6). It is as if praising actual material poverty is a step too far for Matthew, whereas for

---

9   Although much of the same content of what is called the Sermon on the Mount appears in the Gospel of Luke as well as that of Matthew, the location of Jesus' sermon in Luke is not actually a mountain but 'a level place' (Luke 6.17). Furthermore, what appears in one block of teaching in Matthew (Chapters 5–7) is actually spread out in Luke. This divergence is the result of the different theological motivations and purposes of each gospel. Broadly speaking, Matthew's gospel, written for a Jewish-Christian audience, is concerned to show that Jesus is the fulfilment of the Law, a new Moses. Just as Moses received the Law on the mountain, so Jesus teaches the fulfilment of that Law on a mountain, too: 'Do not think I have come to abolish the law or the prophets; I have come not to abolish but to fulfil' (Matthew 5.17). Luke's gospel, written to address the concerns of a community of gentile converts, is not so concerned to present Jesus and his teaching in the light of his Jewish pedigree, hence Luke's lack of concern that Jesus' sermon should be preached on a mountain. Finer nuances in the texts also seem to spring from specific and distinctive theological concerns in each gospel.

Luke, being empty is a sign, a precondition even, of at one and the same time being filled with the fullness of God.

In Matthew's gospel, Jesus continues to advocate such things as refraining from retaliation after being struck on the cheek by voluntarily turning the other cheek towards one's aggressor for the same treatment (Matthew 6.39), and loving and praying for one's enemies rather than hating them (Matthew 6.44). He suggests, furthermore, that entry into the kingdom of heaven is on the basis not simply of mouthing the right words – 'Not everyone who says to me, "Lord, Lord", will enter the kingdom of heaven, but only one who does the will of my Father in heaven' (Matthew 7.21) – but of acting on them, embodying them and making them one's own: 'Everyone then who hears these words of mine and acts on them will be like a wise man who built his house on rock' (Matthew 7.24). The common thread that seems to run through this teaching is that whereas we seem to spend much of our time and energy as human beings in defending our sense of self, by amassing, acquiring and gaining such things – 'material' as well as 'spiritual' – as will build up a sense of self, it is actually in letting go of ourselves that our true self is discovered. The problem with believing that we have a self in this sense that needs protecting is that we are beset by an underlying anxiety and insecurity that this self is constantly under threat of being taken away somehow. It is precisely this fundamental and universal anxiety that Jesus addresses. He invites us, rather like a Zen master, to approach this anxiety as a kind of *kōan*, to let it go, to 'pass through' it, to see that this small self, as it were, lacks real substance, and awaken to the emptiness – which is at the same time the fullness – of who we are.

This is the context of Jesus' teaching about the birds of the air and the lilies of the field. Jesus addresses our all too pervasive human tendency to let worry be our default attitude to life. Worry and anxiety derive ultimately from a belief that we lack what we think we need. In inviting us to look at the birds of the air and the lilies of the field, Jesus invites us to see that everything that they – and by implication, of course, we, too – need is already there, has already been provided. The attitude to life that Jesus is commending is one of total trust and acceptance:

> Therefore do not worry, saying, 'What will we eat?' or 'What will we wear?' For it is the Gentiles who strive for all these things; and indeed your heavenly Father knows that you need all these things. But strive first for the kingdom of God and his righteousness, and all these things will be given to you as well. So do not worry about tomorrow, for tomorrow will bring worries of its own. Today's trouble is enough for today. (Matthew 6.31–34)

This seems to be a counsel of perfection; it runs counter to everything that we have been conditioned to think. So how do we begin to adopt this attitude and approach to life? It is here that the practice of *zazen* can illuminate the matter.

Zazen: letting go of guilt and anxiety

When we sit *zazen*, we become aware of all sorts of thoughts that arise in the mind. Some of these are trivial but others seem to be more deeply rooted. Generally speaking, the thoughts that 'distract' us relate to the past or to the future and, therefore, are often characterised by guilt or anxiety. Guilt arises most obviously as a response to things we have said or done to offend, hurt or diminish others in some way. Even when the one to whom we have caused pain readily forgives us, it is extraordinary how we so often find it difficult to accept that we are forgiven, and so guilt continues to fester within. In some cases, guilt can be the result of conditioning of a particularly brutal and pernicious kind. Those who have been subjected to abuse of one kind or another, for example, especially as children, despite the fact that they themselves are not at fault, often feel guilt and shame. In many cases, such things can take years to see for what they truly are. The overwhelming effect of guilt, however, is that it keeps us firmly entrenched in the past. We have to learn to let it go.

Anxiety has the same kind of effect but in relation to the future. Anxiety arises out of a sense of lack or inadequacy. As the consequence of conditioning in childhood, for example, it may derive from a belief instilled in us that we will never be acceptable unless we measure up to an impossible standard or out-perform everyone else, showing ourselves to be far superior. This can then affect our whole attitude to life, so that we are constantly striving for wealth, power, status or some other such thing, as a way of building up our fragile sense of identity and security against the time when we perceive ourselves to be under threat and at risk of being 'overtaken' by others. It is self-evidently the case, of course, that others may be wealthier, more intelligent, more able, and so on, than we are, but the anxious drive constantly to improve ourselves in relation to others can often stem from a lack of self-acceptance. Just as guilt keeps our attention focused firmly in the past, anxiety focuses our attention on the future and on an unattainable or forever elusive goal. Both deflect our attention from the present, which is where we are, inescapably, at every moment. Living in the present means being present to what is, here and now, to who we are at this moment. Identifying ourselves with guilt or anxiety turns out to be a form of delusion: 'Can any of you by worrying add a single hour to your span of life?' (Matthew 6.27). Can worry itself actually make things different? No. Like guilt, we have to let go of worry and anxiety, too.

As we sit *zazen*, so we begin to distance ourselves from our self-identification with guilt and anxiety, or from anything else with which we identify ourselves for that matter. We allow thoughts to arise but we resist engaging with them and simply let them come and go.

This is where we meet one of those paradoxes which are so characteristic of Zen. We can come to the practice of *zazen* with all sorts of expectations: that the 'sit' will be peaceful, that thoughts will not arise, that we shall 'gain' enlightenment, or that our suffering will cease, and so on. We have to let go even of such expectations, though, and simply let the sit be what it is. It may well be that we try to keep our attention focused on the breath or on some other such thing, but as and when thoughts arise, we acknowledge them, accept them and let them go. However many times we have to go through this process is of no concern or consequence, even if it seems that we are continuously and relentlessly harassed by distracting thoughts. The paradox is that it is by accepting and not resisting what arises that the grip these things have on us begins to be relaxed. This is because we bring to *zazen* something more, something beyond our identification with our thoughts. We bring a compassionate awareness, which embraces, enfolds and accepts everything that arises, whether it be guilt or anxiety or anything else, and which allows the natural expansiveness of who we really are to emerge. This is an expansive awareness, which has been beautifully alluded to in a slightly different context as the sense of 'unknown boundless presence' (Epstein 2013a, p.177), or 'boundless support' (Epstein 2013b).

Jesus' teaching comes from this place of expansive, compassionate awareness, for in this he is identified not with guilt or anxiety, but with God, the ultimate ground of this compassionate awareness, in and through whom every aspect of life, ourselves included, is grounded and supported at every moment. Indeed, when we let go of guilt and anxiety and anything else that we identify with, we discover that God is truly our life as God is Jesus' life, and it is to this truth that Jesus seeks to awaken us.

Why do you call me good?

If Jesus' teaching in the Sermon on the Mount invites us to see and think differently, the encounter between Jesus and a man who approached him to ask what he had to do to inherit eternal life (Mark 10.17–22) does the same, but in a rather disconcerting way on account of the brusqueness of Jesus' response to him. The man addresses Jesus as 'Good Teacher', but Jesus rejects this approach by asking: 'Why do you call me good? No one is good but God alone' (Mark 10.17–18). Why does Jesus act in this way?

We might assume that the man was simply being courteous. Jesus' rebuke, however, is reminiscent of what many might take rather stereotypically to be the manner of many a Zen master, in abruptly dismissing the very first words a student utters in *dokusan*,[10] in an attempt to articulate his or her understanding: 'No, that's not it; go away and come back when you have something sensible to say!' (I hasten to add that this view is a stereotype, though not without some basis in reality in certain instances.) Such abruptness, though, brings us up short, and once we have got over our bruised ego, it forces us to reconsider both who the teacher is and who we are. It calls into question the ideas, thoughts and assumptions we project onto others and, indeed, onto the whole of our experience.

So another possible motive for the way in which the man addressed Jesus might have been to keep Jesus at arm's length, as it were, in order to prevent Jesus from unmasking the games and pretences in which he was habitually involved. 'Good Teacher' could have been intentionally obsequious. Obsequiousness is really a form of manipulation, in which we flatter someone else to distract that person from getting too close to the truth about us. Thus in addressing Jesus as 'good' before asking what he had to do to inherit eternal life, the man might have been hoping that, having been flattered, Jesus would congratulate him with a pat on the back and confirm him in the way he lived his life. In rejecting the man's form of address, Jesus signalled that he was not interested in playing games and rather peremptorily told the man that his question had already been addressed by the commandments. When the man insisted that he had kept them all since his youth, Jesus saw through him with immense compassion, for we read: 'Jesus, looking at him,

_____

10 A (usually fairly brief) one-to-one interview, in which a student discusses his or her practice with the teacher.

loved him and said, "You lack one thing; go, sell what you own, and give the money to the poor, and you will have treasure in heaven; then come, follow me.'" Jesus had hit the nail on the head, for when the man heard what Jesus had to say, 'he was shocked and went away grieving, for he had many possessions' (Mark 10.22; emphasis added).

Jesus was motivated completely by his desire that the man should awaken to the truth of his own condition: the man was rather pleased with himself and appeared to believe that he had every right to be. His pride, however, was itself a kind of possession, which, Jesus told him, had to be relinquished if he truly wanted to know eternal life. His possessive attitude was also clearly expressed in the possessiveness with which he clung to material wealth, for it was this that he was unable to surrender.

When we sit *zazen*, we come face to face with the games we play, with the image we present to the world, and with what we project onto reality. These things have the effect of distorting what is actually 'there', so sitting *zazen* is more than anything else about letting things go rather than acquiring something. It is only then that we can begin to see things clearly. Much of what we think is conditioned by our common experience, more often than not to our disadvantage and to the disadvantage of others, too. We see things through the lens of our conditioning, and it is such distortions that sitting *zazen* enables us little by little to see. Whatever had contributed to the man's conditioning, Jesus held up the fact of his conditioning for him to see and invited him to let it go. This he did by something as seemingly innocent and innocuous as questioning why the man called him good. While the man flinched from facing up to the implications and consequences of his conditioning, Jesus offered him a way of seeing and dealing with it. As far as we know, the man could not face having his world turned on its head, unless at a later stage his discomfort got the better of him.

Beyond binary thinking

The final aspect of Jesus' teaching – with which I briefly wish to engage in the context of this chapter – as having the capacity to enable us to see differently, is the way Jesus resisted responding to his opponents in a dualistic frame of mind. On so many occasions, the gospels show us that his detractors set out to trap him by clever words. This they did by asking him questions, such that however he answered, his reply would inevitably convict him. In this sense, his enemies, largely, in this instance, the religious authorities, were incredibly clever, but they operated on the basis of a binary way of thinking.

So, when Jesus was asked whether people should pay taxes to the emperor or not (Matthew 22.15–22), Jesus knew full well that a positive answer would align him with the forces of Roman oppression and occupation, whereas a negative one would enable others to label him a dissident, at odds with the authorities as a subversive influence and, therefore, to be denounced – hypocritically in the case of the Pharisees. Jesus dealt with this by refusing to answer the question in the way that it was presented. He called for a coin used to pay tax and asked whose head was imprinted on the coin. 'The emperor's,' came the reply. Jesus said to them, 'Give, therefore, to the emperor the things that are the emperor's and to God the things that are God's' (Matthew 22.21).

The most moving example of how Jesus responds in this manner is in the incident in the Gospel of John, where the Scribes and Pharisees throw at Jesus' feet a woman who had been caught in the act of adultery (John 8.1–11). The Mosaic Law demanded that the penalty for such an act was death by stoning. Jesus was asked for his view as to what was to be done with the woman. Jesus and his adversaries knew full well that if he had advocated turning a blind eye, he would have been seen as disregarding the requirements of the Law, thereby depriving himself of any legitimate authority. If, however, he had counselled stoning, he would have condemned the woman alone – and, in accordance with the Law, not the man in question – to a vicious and vengeful death, thus revealing a lack of compassion.

Jesus' response was legendary. He knelt down on the ground, doodled in the sand for a while, and then enjoined whoever was without sin to cast the first stone. The important thing to note is that Jesus rejected neither the sin nor the concern for justice, in much the same way that Bodhidharma dismissed neither Huike's mind nor his suffering, but rather transcended the duality by acknowledging and giving place to both. Jesus pointed to and showed a different way of seeing by bringing to bear on the situation a compassionate awareness that embraced opposites and dualities and yet went beyond them.

Summary: letting go and seeing differently

This chapter has been concerned with showing how human beings might find a way home from the exile that seems to characterise much of our experience. The story of Bodhidharma putting the mind to rest demonstrated that the path home lies in allowing the way we see things to be changed, so that we wake up to who we really are and realise that we are always at home already. Similarly, the brief exploration of some of Jesus' teaching showed that Jesus also invites a different way of seeing, brought about largely by an attitude to life of letting go. It is paradoxically by letting go of ourselves that we wake up to ourselves. The unwillingness or resistance to following this path is what contributes to our suffering. In Jesus' case, this is what led ultimately to his crucifixion. It is to this general direction that we turn in Part 2 of the book.

The volatile circumstances of Jesus' life

Jesus was born into a political that religious institution. Despite believing that they were loved and chosen by God for the purpose of embodying and revealing his life and character of God for the benefit of the whole world, his people had been continuously subjected to one tragedy-ending and disappointment after another. Early on in their history they had been taken into slavery in Egypt. Many years later in their later history, Babylon had invaded and besieged the northern kingdom of Israel and then, in the not too distant past, had taken to Babylon the children of Israel. The Babylonian army not only deported the wealthy of the population into exile in Babylon, but also destroyed the things that were the most sacred and symbolic emblems of their identity, the temple and the king's palace.

Although Cyrus of Persia had made it possible for the exiles to return towards the end of the century, the country had subsequently found itself first at the mercy of the Greeks, and then, in 63 BCE, the Romans had conquered Jerusalem and subjected the Jewish kingdom to their rule and dominion. Throughout almost their entire history the Jewish people had experienced insecurity, powerlessness and suffering on a colossal scale. It is not surprising, therefore, that they longed for the time when their situation would be reversed, and they would finally be established in peace and security, confident in who they were as the chosen people and able to live in freedom and prosperity. Jesus was born into a situation where nerves were tight and antennae were alert to detect anyone who might look like a possible saviour. Anyone who promised to overthrow the Romans and restore the kingdom of Israel

PART 2

Clarifying the Great Matter

Chapter 3

Taking Responsibility

Two gathas

Most Zen groups, when they gather for a period of *zazen*, are likely to frame their time of sitting by reciting two *gathas* or chants. The first, the *Gatha of Atonement*, is chanted by everyone together in unison on a monotone at the beginning of a sit, and the second, the *Evening Gatha*, is usually recited by a single voice to conclude the time of sitting. Both *gathas* are relatively short, but their significance for Zen practice cannot be overstated. The words of the *Gatha of Atonement* are as follows:

> All harmful karma ever created by me of old on account of my beginningless greed, hatred and ignorance, born of my conduct, speech and thought, I atone for it now.

The *Evening Gatha* is this:

Let me respectfully remind you, life and death are of supreme importance. Time swiftly passes by and opportunity is lost. Each of us should strive to awaken, awaken. Take heed, do not squander your life.

At the heart of each of these *gathas* is the notion of taking responsibility for our own lives, and it is to this aspect of Zen practice that we now turn.

The need to take responsibility for our lives

It may seem slightly odd to suggest that attention should be drawn to the need to take responsibility for our own lives, but a moment's reflection would probably lead us to conclude that few of us live fully in the awareness of the sheer reality of our lives. Many of us, in one way or another, live on automatic pilot, so to speak, simply going through the motions. In one sense, this is not entirely to be lamented. Some decisions, for example, would be thoroughly burdensome if we had to make the same decision time and time again. The commitment to sitting *zazen* is an example in point. The decision, made in principle, that I will sit *zazen* each day, regardless of whether I feel like it or not, removes from me the burden of having to make that decision every time. There may well be occasions, of course, when I really do not feel like it. It is important to be aware of such feelings and dispositions, but in relation to a commitment to sit *zazen* daily, they are superseded by a prior decision that anticipates and deals with such misgivings in advance. To suggest that this is like being on automatic pilot is simply to say that *zazen* is an indispensable part of my life.

There is no need to make that fundamental decision every time I consider whether to sit *zazen*.

There are other aspects of our lives, however, of which we are unaware of the need to take responsibility, or for which we are disinclined to do so. This has to do largely with our conditioning. From the moment we are born, we are inducted into a way of living over which we have no choice, and yet which shapes our way of engaging with the world. The obvious locus for this is in our immediate family relationships, whatever shape they might take. We imbibe the values, mores and worldviews of those who raise us as children and, for some, the need to question such things simply does not arise. The same is true of the broader societal and cultural context into which we are inducted. We can live our lives unquestioningly in accordance with the assumptions, beliefs and values which we inherit from an age-old historical tradition, whether that be rooted in Christianity, Islam, Buddhism, liberalism, communism or some other such thing.

Again, in principle, there is nothing wrong with this, indeed it is necessary. Unless we were shaped and formed by something, it is difficult to see how it would be possible to engage with the world at all. Thus, while basic codes of even seemingly trivial behaviour will vary from family to family, country to country, and culture to culture, without them there would be chaos. It would be as if my decision in principle to sit *zazen* each day were replicated in relation to every aspect of life by everyone, everywhere, at every moment. Some conditioning in this sense is necessary and desirable for life to function at all.

There are, however, more sinister dimensions to conditioning. If a child grows up in a family where behaviour, conversations and interactions are habitually characterised by verbal abuse and aggression, for example, that child will initially assume that speaking to others in the same manner is simply normal and acceptable. The fact that the child will subsequently encounter the disapproval of others, whether at school, if not before, or elsewhere, does not alter the fact that the child will have unconsciously absorbed the way or relating and speaking to others, which was common currency for them in family life.

Much the same thing, of course, can occur at a societal level. The history of the Civil Rights Movement in the United States of America, or of the institutional racial segregation and discrimination known as *Apartheid* in South Africa, to cite obvious examples, shows that if a certain constituency of the population is brought up to believe that some people of a different racial background are inferior, the consequences are horrendous and long-lasting. No matter how much logic and reason might be applied in the attempt to persuade people to see things differently, it is evident that such conditioning runs very deep indeed, and changing it becomes a herculean task. Some people simply remain blind to it. This is not to say, however, that all are completely unable to see and rise above their conditioning. In the USA and in South Africa, many white people aligned themselves with those who were oppressed because their skin was a different colour, and advocated their cause, often at great cost to themselves. Racial prejudice still seems to linger in both countries, nevertheless, despite extraordinary advances for the better.

When we resist waking up to the fact of our conditioning, for whatever reason, we live and act without self-awareness and self-knowledge, and remain in a state of delusion. Our every thought and action springs from somewhere deep in the unconscious, and we may not even be aware of the effect that the way we live has on the lives of others. When something does happen that causes us to wake up, though, the initial effect can be shattering. It can seem that our lives have been something of a lie, that we have been living from the wrong place, as it were. We begin to see the harm that our conditioning has had on us and others by the way it has blinded us to other aspects of reality, other dimensions of experience, other ways of looking at things. So, too, do we begin to perceive all the psychological, emotional and intellectual strategies and defences that we have employed to protect ourselves – invariably against hurt in childhood – and simply allowing the reality of our woundedness to surface can be profoundly painful. This is part of what it means to take responsibility for our lives, though. Taking responsibility for my life means accepting the totality of my life as it is, and all that has contributed to what it is at this very moment.

One of the most serious obstacles to doing this lies in the impulse and inclination to blame others for the way our lives are. The child who has been abused, or the person of colour who has been subjected to prejudice and discrimination, has every reason to feel aggrieved. The impact of what has been suffered must never be underestimated, dismissed or repressed, but somehow has to be acknowledged, accepted and embraced as part of who we are. The tendency to blame, however, shifts the responsibility for our lives as they are now at this moment to somewhere else, deprives us of our inherent freedom and personal integrity, and perpetuates negative cycles of conditioning.[1] For the plain fact of the matter is that we ourselves are not the only ones who have been conditioned. Every single person has also been conditioned, and their actions, just like our own, spring from their own conditioning. The important thing is that we all hear the call to wake up to the reality of our own lives and take responsibility for them as they are now. This is what the *Gatha of Atonement* and the *Evening Gatha* invite us to do every time they are chanted.

In the Christian context, atonement is the term given to refer to what Christ is understood to have achieved on the cross. Christians believe that through his death, God, humanity and creation are reconciled. From the Zen perspective, atonement might be thought of as being reconciled to our lives as they are. Such reconciliation, of course, necessarily involves waking up to the truth of who we are, seeing into our true nature, and being at one with it. Such at-one-ment, however, embraces the whole of reality and, therefore, includes everyone and everything else. This is what our lives are when we see them for what they are. It is for this reason that when entering the *zendo*, a bow is made not only in the direction of the Buddha, but also to one's mat and cushion before sitting down to take one's place. Bowing to the mat and cushion is a way of taking responsibility for what occurs during a period

---

1   This is exactly what the story of the Fall seeks to show in Genesis 3. When God enquires of the man why he is naked and whether he has eaten of the forbidden fruit, he implicitly shifts the responsibility on to the woman, by replying that it was she gave who him the fruit to eat – and is, therefore to blame – and she in turn blames the serpent for tricking her (Genesis 3.11–13). The whole biblical story shows the repercussions that follow from this, including the longing for and coming of redemption.

of *zazen*, and acknowledging that the whole of one's life is, so to speak, present on the mat. This includes all the many causes, conditions and consequences – *karma* – that constitute our lives as they are at this very moment.

Taking responsibility for our lives, as well as recognising the way that we have perpetuated 'all harmful *karma*' as a consequence of the three poisons of 'greed, hatred and ignorance', also includes what the great Zen Master Dōgen (1200–1253) refers to as 'clarifying the great matter'. This concerns the quest to discover what life really is, and is a matter of life and death: 'Life and death are of supreme importance. Each of us should strive to awaken, awaken. Take heed, do not squander your life.'[2]

What I should like to do as this chapter proceeds, therefore, is to pursue all this in relation to two things. First, the opera, *Parsifal*, by Richard Wagner (1813–1883) and, second, Dōgen's own search to clarify the great matter. *Parsifal* might seem a rather unlikely choice of subject for a book such as this, but I hope its attraction in this context will become clear as the chapter unfolds. The fact that the opera is clearly indebted to both Christian and Buddhist influences is fortuitous for the purpose of what I should like to say, but this is not the primary issue I intend to address, although I shall sketch out something of the lie of the land. Of more significance is that in the central character of Parsifal himself, there is an archetypal portrayal of how we wake up to our own lives, take responsibility for them, and then put them to use in the service of atonement and reconciliation. As far as Dōgen is concerned, justification is scarcely needed. He is, after all,

---

2   See the *Evening Gatha* at the start of this chapter.

one of the greatest figures in the history of Zen, and it is precisely in seeking to 'clarify the great matter' that he can be seen to be taking responsibility for his life. As such, he is the most encouraging example and illuminating guide. First, though, let us turn to *Parsifal*.

Parsifal – setting the scene

Parsifal, for which Wagner drew substantial inspiration from the medieval German romance, *Parzival*, written by the poet Wolfram von Eschenbach in the early years of the thirteenth century, was Wagner's last completed opera (1882) and, as such, represents the pinnacle and consummation of his artistic career. All of his operas inhabit a mythical realm and deal with the biggest and most challenging questions in life. The length of his operas also matches the magnitude of the concerns they address. They work on us primarily at a subliminal level, which is why they are both endlessly evocative and also forever open to a diversity of interpretation. The adulation of Wagner's music by Hitler, as well as some of the unfortunate views that Wagner himself held about the Jewish race, means that, for some, Wagner's creations are irredeemably tainted and unworthy of attention. Some Christians, too, while acknowledging that the legend of the Grail emerges in a Christian context, perceive Wagner's treatment of Christian themes to be highly unorthodox. Others, though, are less concerned. Richard Bell, for example, suggests that it is 'not only possible to integrate *Parsifal* into a Christian theological outlook, but also to study *Parsifal* such that it presents distinctive theological insights...even though there are some "unorthodox" elements in it' (Bell 2013, p.5).[3]

The influence of Buddhism on *Parsifal* is acknowledged by all, but as is the case with assessments of *Parsifal's* Christian content, what Wagner understood about Buddhism may be considered in some ways to be misguided, and it will be helpful to address this here. Wagner was introduced to Buddhism through his reading of the philosopher, Arthur Schopenhauer (1788–1860). As a result of reading the philosopher's *Die Welt als Wille und Vorstellung* (*The World as Will and Representation*) during the last few months of 1854, Wagner was inspired to start making sketches in 1856 for an opera – *Die Sieger* (*The Victors*) – based on the life of Buddha. The initial sketches never came to anything more than that, but evidence of Wagner's engagement with Buddhism can be seen in the tetralogy, *Der Ring des Nibelungen* (*The Ring of the Nibelungs*),[4] which took him 26 years to complete from 1848 to 1874, *Tristan und Isolde* (*Tristan and Isolde*), composed between 1857 and 1859, and *Parsifal*, which he first conceived in 1857, but did not complete until 1882.

---

3   For other studies of *Parsifal* which deal with the Christian elements, see Becket (1981, especially pp.129–149); Kienzle (2010, pp.81–130), who suggests that *Parsifal* is not a Christian music drama, if it is to be considered as 'reinforcing the dogmas of the Church', but that it is 'if we take the interwoven paths of medieval and modern mysticism seriously as components of the Christian tradition' (Kienzle 2010, p.130); and Mastrogiovanni (2014), who is overwhelmingly supportive of a positive Christian interpretation: 'Wagner is saying to us that he believed that in Christ all are absolved and atoned, all races, religions and castes, all are welcome to be united with the Divine' (Mastrogiovanni 2014, p.187).

4   The four operas that constitute the *Ring Cycle* are: *Das Rheingold* (*The Rhinegold*), *Die Walküre* (*The Valkyrie*), *Siegfried*, and *Die Götterdämmerung* (*The Twilight of the Gods*).

Among the themes with which these three works are concerned is desire: the desire for power (*The Ring*), the desire for union in love (*Tristan and Isolde*), and the desire for redemption (*Parsifal*). The word 'desire' in the Buddhist context is liable to significant misinterpretation. As far as the Four Noble Truths are concerned, *tanhā* – craving or, indeed, desire – is the cause of suffering. Desire is the product of the will, and so Schopenhauer argued that if suffering is to be brought to an end, it can only be achieved by the extinction of the will and its desires. Caution needs to be taken here, though, for the matter is slightly more nuanced than that. Craving is not *exactly* the same as desire. As we noted in the first chapter, Siddhārtha Gautama's own search for enlightenment was itself motivated by desire. Had it not been, there would have been nothing to initiate his search in the first place. Schopenhauer's misreading of Buddhism was the result of misunderstanding the nature of the will and of *Nirvana*. There is something more, though, and this has to do with what is perceived to be the state that arises as a result of the extinction of desire:

The Sanskrit word *Nirvana* comes from two words, *nir* and *vana*. *Nir* means 'not' or 'no,' and *vana* means 'craving' or 'desire'. Thus *Nirvana*, literally translated, means 'no craving', or 'no desire'. Schopenhauer understood this etymologically. But he did not understand the true nature of the state attained by having no desire. It is not, as Schopenhauer thought a final nothing or state of oblivion, nor is it the extinction of being or consciousness. When Buddhism says that '*Nirvana* is extinction,' it means that *Nirvana* is the extinction of the illusion of a separate self. It is the extinction of the flames of greed, hate and delusion. It is emancipation from the wheel of birth and death, what Christianity calls eternal life. It is eternal meditation forever at one with the great *Dharmakāya*,[5] the great eternally shining light. The Buddha specifically said, 'Nirvana is the highest bliss.' It is not an eternal sleep. (Schofield 2007, pp.9–10)

---

5 According the *Trikāya* doctrine in Mahāyāna Buddhism, there are three 'Buddha bodies': 1) *Dharmakāya*, which is the absolute, the ultimate, the unborn, the essence of the universe, the basis of reality, the ungraspable, the unfathomable, that which is beyond existence and non-existence, the emptiness from which all phenomena emanate; 2) *Nirmānakāya*, the relative, that which is manifested as the form of an earthly, physical body, subject to old age, sickness and death; the one who teaches the Dharma and leads others to enlightenment; 3) *Sambhogakāya*, the interface or relationship between the absolute and the relative, the body that experiences the fruits of practice and the bliss and enjoyment of enlightenment, clarity and knowledge. These three bodies are not to be conceived as separate, though – they are one. On the basis of this, it is possible to say that, at the very least, there is a resonance with or an affinity between this doctrine and the doctrine of the Trinity in Christian theology, which affirms that the Father is the unknowable, unmanifested source and ground, who manifests and knows himself and makes himself known in the Son, both of whom are at one in the Spirit, in much the same way that the twentieth-century Christian pioneers in India proposed a synergy between the Christian experience of God as Trinity and the Hindu experience of God as *Saccidananda*: *Sat* – Being (Father); *Cit* – Consciousness (Son); *Ānanda* – Bliss (Spirit). In connection with this, see du Boulay 1998, p.146: 'They [Jules Monchanin and Henri le Saux] called it Saccidananda Ashram (the Hindu name for the Godhead, from the Sanskrit words *sat* "being", *cit* "awareness", *ānanda* "bliss"), the implicit message being that the Hindu quest for God, enshrined in this ancient word, finds its parallel in the Christian Trinity.' For further theological explanation of this, see Abhishiktānanda (1984, pp.177–186) and Griffiths (1991, pp.118–122).

There is no doubt that some of these ideas found their way into *Parsifal*, which is very much about the suffering that is caused by desire, and its redemption by addressing its causes. It would be easy – though misguided – to interpret the underlying message of *Parsifal* to be that all desire has to be extinguished completely for suffering to come to an end. This, however, would be to ignore the obvious point that the outcome of *Parsifal's* spiritual journey is not simply the extinction of desire, but the transformation of desire into compassion, in order to bring redemption to all who suffer. As well the character of Parsifal himself being a Christ figure, he is also a *Bodhisattva* – one who is capable of attaining the 'final state', but who foregoes entering into it until all have been saved. *Parsifal* is, therefore, ultimately life-affirming and life-giving, not life-denying.

With this important clarification in mind, we can now turn to the story of *Parsifal* itself for what it can show us about what it is to be asleep to the reality of life, what it is to wake up to it, and what it is to take responsibility for it. Although it is necessary to give a simple outline of the story, I am concerned to show the significance of just two particular moments in the opera. The first has to do with Parsifal's inability to see, to understand, what is unfolding before his eyes, and, therefore, his failure to take responsibility for his life. The second concerns his moment of awakening, the point at which he does, indeed, truly take responsibility for his life.

Parsifal in brief

Wagner is never uncomplicated, and we need to understand something of the background to the opera before it actually begins. According to legend, two holy relics had been passed into the safe keeping of Titurel: the spear which was used to wound Christ on the cross and the Grail or chalice used at the Last Supper, and into which Christ's wounds had bled while he hung on the cross. For the purposes of guarding the spear and the Grail – which also had miraculous powers – Titurel had formed an order of chivalry.

Klingsor had longed to be admitted to this order, but, for whatever reason, had not been elected. Determined to prove his worthiness, Klingsor had castrated himself in an attempt to demonstrate his purity.[6] For this act of self-mutilation, he had received nothing but the scorn and ridicule of the knights, in angry response to which he had vowed revenge. This he had put into action by turning to sorcery, transforming a barren desert into a magic garden, and populating it with beautiful women, whose task it was to seduce unsuspecting knights. Many had been trapped and imprisoned by Klingsor, whose fervent wish it remained, nevertheless, to become the guardian of the Holy Grail.

Titurel had abdicated from his position in old age and his son, Amfortas, had been chosen by the order to succeed him. Having tried to destroy Klingsor, Amfortas had fallen prey to Klingsor's sorcery, and had himself been seduced by Kundry, who was said to have laughed at Christ while he hung on the cross. Although Amfortas had managed to escape from the clutches of Kundry and Klingsor, Klingsor

---

6   Perhaps this is to be taken as a rather oblique implication that Klingsor was rejected by the Grail community on account of uncontrolled or misdirected sexual desire. Klingsor is entirely Wagner's creation and not that of Wolfram von Eschenbach.

had managed to grasp the spear from Amfortas and wound him with it. Following this, it had been prophesied that healing could only come by means of a pure fool made wise by compassion. Until that time, Amfortas remained in continuous pain and agony, made all the worse whenever he was called on to officiate at the ritual of the Holy Grail.

When the curtain rises, Gurnemanz, the most senior knight in the order, is recounting this history to two of the other knights, while attempting to rouse them from sleep, in order that they might fulfil their duty in guarding the sanctuary. As they pray together, two more knights enter to inform them of the imminent arrival of Amfortas, who is coming to the lake to bathe his wound, and for which Kundry has brought ointment from Arabia. It is at this point that Gurnemanz alludes to the prophecy that had emanated from the Grail itself, that healing and redemption would only be possible with the arrival of an innocent fool: 'Durch Mitleid wissend der reine Tor; harre sein, den ich erkor' ('Made wise through compassion the innocent fool; wait for him, the one I summon') (Wagner 1962, p.44). The knights start to repeat the prophecy, but before they can complete it, shouts are heard in the direction of the lake. A wild swan has been shot and wounded by a stranger, who turns out to be Parsifal. As the swan flies from the lake and falls to the ground and dies, Parsifal is brought on by knights who have apprehended him.

Gurnemanz, enraged by this gratuitous act of violence, asks him if he was responsible. Parsifal boasts that if something flies, he shoots it. Gurnemanz forces Parsifal to look at the lifeless body, a swan which had been in search of its mate, and asks what possible motive there could have been to harm the swan. Parsifal replies that he does not know, but in a moment of remorse, which as yet he appears not fully to comprehend, snaps his bow. In response to further questioning from Gurnemanz, it emerges that Parsifal knows little about his origins or even his name, except that his mother was called Herzeleide – Heart's Sorrow or Heartache.

Kundry, who has been listening all along, and who is strangely party to knowledge about Parsifal's history, of which even Parsifal himself is ignorant, then tells him that his father had been killed in battle as a knight, for which reason his mother had forbidden him ever to pick up a sword, lest he meet the same fate as his father. At this, Parsifal recalls that long ago he had seen a group of knights riding through the forest and had decided on the spur of the moment to follow them. Kundry informs him that this act of abandoning his mother, without even turning back to bid her farewell, had caused her to die of grief.

The scene changes to the interior of the Castle of the Grail, where the ceremony of the Holy Grail is shortly to take place. The Holy Grail has life-enhancing powers and during the course of the ceremony, the holy blood mystically enters Amfortas's body, causing his own sinful blood to be expelled from his body through his wound, resulting in unbearable agony. When Parsifal is unable to show any understanding of what he has witnessed, Gurnemanz sends Parsifal on his way, angrily telling him that he is no more than a fool.

The second act takes place entirely in Klingsor's castle. Parsifal has been wandering rather aimlessly for years, but as he approaches Klingsor's castle, Klingsor sees an opportunity and summons his knights to fight him. Kundry watches over Parsifal and enables him to defeat them, but then, enslaved to Klingsor's demands, proceeds to entrap and seduce Parsifal. Having failed to respond to the charms of the flower maidens, Parsifal is now entranced by Kundry, who calls him by his name. When he enquires as to how she knows his name, she reveals that she has known him since before he was born, that she witnessed him when he was in the womb, and how his father had decreed his name, but had died before his mother gave birth.

She then proceeds to recount the story of how his mother sought to protect him from harm, how she loved him, and how she was heart-stricken when, one day, Parsifal had simply left home without saying goodbye. On hearing this, Parsifal is filled with grief and announces that he himself was responsible for his mother's death. As Kundry lures him ever more deeply into her embrace, she tries to persuade Parsifal that she can heal his pain and grief and help him to understand his mother's love for him, by giving him the blessing and farewell greeting that his mother was never able to give him – with a kiss. As they kiss, truth dawns, and Parsifal intuitively understands the cause of Amfortas's pain and resists any further advances from Kundry. He requests that she take him to Amfortas, and she replies that if he will stay with her for just one more hour, she will do so. When Parsifal declines, Kundry curses him to a life of wandering without ever finding the Grail. Klingsor appears as soon as Kundry calls him and, in an attempt to thwart Parsifal's escape, hurls his spear at him. Parsifal manages to catch the spear and, as he makes the sign of the cross with it, Klingsor's castle disintegrates.

At the beginning of the third and final act, Gurnemanz, now living as a hermit, finds Kundry half-dead. Whereas she was once wild and uncontrollable, she is now calm and eager only to serve. As Parsifal advances, spear in hand, Gurnemanz admonishes him for being armed in a sacred place and on such a holy day, for it is Good Friday. On recognising Parsifal and the spear, Gurnemanz informs Parsifal that Titurel is dead, that the community of knights is on the point of collapse, and that Amfortas is refusing them access to the Grail. Parsifal blames himself for this turn of events. Kundry washes Parsifal's feet and is then anointed by Gurnemanz, after which Parsifal baptises Kundry.

As a bell begins to toll, the whole community of knights is summoned to the Castle of the Grail. Amfortas is brought in to lie before the Grail shrine and Titurel's coffin. The knights demand that he unveil the Grail, but he resists and begs them to kill him, in order that his own suffering and the shame that he has brought on the order might be ended. At this point, Parsifal steps forward and announces that only the spear which he carries in his hand can bring healing. He touches Amfortas's wound, which is instantly healed. Parsifal then commands the unveiling of the Grail, Kundry, released from her curse, falls lifeless to the ground, and a dove descends and hovers over Parsifal.

Waking up and taking responsibility for one's life

Christians will immediately recognise much of the symbolism of the opera, particularly that of the third act. It is not with the final act, however, that I am primarily concerned for the purposes of this book, but with the other two. As was mentioned earlier in this chapter, there are two key moments, which relate, first, to the experience of being in an unawakened state and, second, to waking up to the reality of one's life. It is in the first act that we see Parsifal blissfully unaware of his actions or their effect. In the second, it is as Kundry kisses him that he wakes up and sees and understands not only his own life, but also that of Amfortas and, by implication, those of all who suffer, which is all of us. Let us consider, then, what these two moments signify.

The first thing to notice about Parsifal's action in killing the swan is its sheer gratuitousness: '*Im Fluge treff ich, was fliegt*' ('*I hit in flight all that flies*'). There is no awareness that the swan is a sentient being, no sense of what it might mean to the community of the Grail or to anyone else. Parsifal's actions are characterised not only by ignorance and a lack of awareness, but also by an arrogance and bravado, as if he has something to prove. In his disregard for the consequences of his actions for anyone else, he shows himself to be egocentric. His world centres on his own desires and wishes. This is borne out by the unthinking way in which he deserted his mother, without any concern for how she might react.

The second thing to notice, then, is Parsifal's complete lack of empathy and compassion. Not only does he almost completely fail to empathise with the swan as a living being, he also fails to empathise in any way at all with Amfortas. The path of awakening to the suffering of others is, not least, by being aware of our own woundedness. Parsifal has disowned any sense of his own pain, though. It is only in the second act, during the process of being seduced, that Parsifal becomes truly aware of the reality and impact of loss: of his father before he was even born, and of his mother as a result of grief.

There is, however, a glimmer of light in the first act and that has to do with Parsifal's breaking of his bow. Although he has not awakened to the full horror of his senseless killing of the swan, there is some remorse there, even though he seems unable fully to understand or explain it. He begins, nevertheless, to awaken to his own moral responsibility. The sadness, however, is that at this stage, he is unable to make the connection between the pain of the swan and that of Amfortas. But, then, he is innocent and lacking in the breadth and depth of life experience.

In Zen terms, he is consumed, without necessarily knowing it, by the three poisons of greed, hatred and ignorance. Greed denotes the tendency to grasp, the desire to possess. The killing of the swan is, in itself, Parsifal's attempt to possess it for himself by demonstrating his power over it. Hatred has to do with the rejection of anything that might have a claim on our ego and seeks to set it in its rightful place. The killing of the swan represents Parsifal's disregard of the claim on us of all sentient beings to be treated with reverence and respect, as, indeed, we expect ourselves to be treated. Parsifal rejects this in favour of giving full rein to his need to demonstrate his power and strength. Ignorance has to do with the lack of understanding of who we truly are – as not being a separate, isolated self, but deeply interconnected with everything. Ignorance gives rise to delusion and Parsifal shows this by failing to see his connectedness with the swan as a living, breathing, sentient being. It is not until he finds himself in the arms of Kundry that he realises how much he has been in thrall to the three poisons and finally wakes up to the reality of his own life and begins to take responsibility for it.

It is Parsifal's rejection of Kundry in the second act that gives rise to the notion in some quarters that it is only the extinction of all desire – including sexual desire – that will bring an end to suffering. This is a misreading of the situation, though, for it is far more subtle and nuanced than that. The issue is not so much the eradication of all desire but its appropriate direction. Parsifal awakens because he begins to see all sorts of hidden connections in his life, people, deeds and events, which seem to have been relegated to the unconscious, either because they were impediments to the drives of his ego, or because they were too painful for him to face.

There would seem to be an inescapable connection between Parsifal's bravado and his experience of loss. Although he never knew his father, the absence of his father can scarcely be said to have been without impact on him. Just as Siddhārtha Gautama clearly experienced the loss of his mother when he was just days old, without being aware of the full effect that this had on him, much the same must surely be said about Parsifal. His bravado seems to be an unconscious attempt to compensate for this. His killing of the swan suggests the projection of the pain of his loss onto another being, in the attempt to deflect the awareness of his own pain away from himself. There is a partial breaking through of the light of awareness when Parsifal snaps his bow, but this glimmer of awakening does not illuminate Parsifal's understanding sufficiently for him to understand Amfortas's pain. It is only as Kundry recounts the story of his childhood that the possibility of awakening in all its fullness occurs.

It is significant that it is not so much his own loss to which Kundry draws Parsifal's attention, but that of his mother. It is as he hears of the grief which led to his mother's death that he begins to see the impact of his own actions on her. He begins to awaken to the suffering of others, aided, perhaps, by the intuitive connection with his own unarticulated grief at never having known his father. Kundry's seductive power lies in her promise to take the pain away rather than expose him to it. The kiss that she proffers Parsifal purports to be that of a mother but, when mixed up with sexual desire at the same time, it becomes a confusing snare that needs to be disentangled. It would have been so easy for Parsifal to have responded by allowing himself to be drawn further into Kundry's designs, for this would have promised, no doubt, to have been a pleasurable experience, bringing momentary relief and distraction from his suffering. It would have been no more than that, though, for the underlying pain would still have been there. It was only by accepting the reality of suffering that it could be transformed.

Parsifal cannot have known consciously that Amfortas's downfall had been precisely what Parsifal faced at that moment, but he knew intuitively that it was Amfortas's misdirected desire, as potentially it was his own, too, as he was held in Kundry's embrace, that had caused him so much pain and suffering. The catalyst for Parsifal's waking up to and taking responsibility for his own life was his newly dawned compassion for Amfortas, his realisation that they were fellow sufferers, along with all sentient beings. Parsifal's compassion is then demonstrated in action in the third act, as he realises that the consequence of his awakening was to help relieve the suffering that affected the whole community of the Grail, and bring regeneration and restoration of life to the chivalric order.

Karma and responsibility

The story of Parsifal is supremely one of waking up to the challenge of taking responsibility for our own lives. It shows the state of somnolence in which we all live to a degree, but also the way in which we are stirred out of that soporific state by life itself. To an extent, our conditioning anaesthetises us against the raw reality of life. But, as that rawness begins to impinge itself on us, not least by allowing the full weight of suffering to be brought to bear on us, we are broken open, and the possibility of compassion begins to arise. And this is wisdom.

Wisdom and compassion lie together at the heart of Zen, but how does this relate to *karma*? How do we begin to take responsibility for our lives, even those aspects of our lives which are the result of conditioning, and over which we had no influence or control in the first place? Isn't *karma* just a fatalistic way in which one thing leads to another, regardless of what we do? And if that is so, why should we take responsibility for it?

The essential principle of *karma* is that actions have causes and consequences. It is generally assumed that good deeds have positive effects and bad deeds negative ones. Thus the situations in which we find ourselves at any one time are understood to be the result of a variety of deeds – good or bad – in the past, and our actions in the present contribute to future outcomes. In one sense, therefore, our capacity to influence things one way or another might seem to be limited or even non-existent. This is not necessarily the case, though.

One of the truths that *Parsifal* shows is that we are all immersed in a complex web of inter-relationships, of some of which we are completely unaware. I suggested that some of Parsifal's actions and behaviour were the result of things in his past, of which he had no knowledge, the absence of his father being the primary instance. It is also the case that he was born into a culture of chivalry, in which there were certain expectations of how young men were to live their lives. This was simply part of his conditioning. Until his moment of awakening, he acted blindly and in ignorance. Once awakened, though, he became aware of the reality of freedom: he could choose how to respond. It was precisely as he felt the strength of desire in Kundry's arms that the possibility of choice and responsibility emerged. His choice was made not without struggle, but choice it was.

It is often assumed that the principle of *karma* is thoroughly deterministic, but it is not. From a positive point of view it affirms two things. First, that we are not separate, isolated individuals, but inescapably related to everyone and everything else. Seeing this is partly what is involved in seeing into our true nature. It is when we act in the misguided and deluded belief that we are separate and completely in control of our own individual destiny that we are most liable to the negative effects of *karma*. Second, therefore, awakening to the truth that everything is our self opens up to us the startling realisation that we can choose how to act, that we can influence the consequences of our actions for the better, that we can assume responsibility for our own lives. It is as we die to our egocentric, separate selves, that we begin to turn the negative effects of *karma* in a positive direction. While we need to be realistic about the extent to which our actions can be entirely positive, it is also the case that we often seriously underestimate the effects of our actions. Acknowledging all the past effects that have made our lives what they are at this very moment, whether we have contributed personally and intentionally to those effects or not, and simply accepting it all for what it is, is the way we take responsibility for our lives and live in true freedom.

What I have tried to show thus far is that *Parsifal* can take us a long way in the direction of seeing and understanding this. *Parsifal*, though, is a work of the imagination, so let us turn now to an actual, historical life, that of Zen Master Dōgen. There are, indeed, certain similarities between Dōgen and Parsifal, largely in terms of the karmic effects of the loss of parents at an early age. Dōgen's life took a very different direction, though, and the challenge to take responsibility for his own life came in the form of the urgent need to 'clarify the great matter'.

Dōgen

Eihei Dōgen is one of the greatest and most influential figures in Zen. Born into an aristocratic family in Kyoto, Japan, his father died in 1202, when he was just two years of age, and his mother in 1207, when he was seven, but not before she had suggested that he become a monk 'to seek the truth of Buddhism and strive to relieve the tragic sufferings of humanity', which, indeed, he did (Kim 2004, p.19). Little could she have known that it would be her own death that would awaken his own search for enlightenment:

> The loss of his beloved mother when he was only seven threw him into deep sorrow. As he watched the clouds of incense rise in the Takao Temple, he understood the coming-to-be and passing away of all things. The longing

for enlightenment was awakened in his breast. (Dumoulin 2005b, p.52; see p.106, n.5 for details of the source)

Dōgen was evidently extremely intelligent and spiritually sensitive, but life as a monk left him feeling restless. In the first place, he considered Buddhism to have become corrupted, and the monasteries were in thrall both to the court nobility and to the warrior class. Over the course of time, monasteries and other religious institutions had become extremely wealthy as a result of acquiring vast estates without the need to pay tax. Furthermore, the larger monasteries had armies comprising what were called *sōhei* or 'armed monastics', who were employed to solve conflicts with other monastic communities and the government. This involved sometimes destroying rival monasteries and presenting petitions to the imperial court by force. As Kim puts it:

> Although the wealth, prestige and power of some established monasteries undoubtedly increased, their moral, intellectual and religious life was dangerously disintegrating. Armed monastics were very active during *Dōgen's* lifetime, and their entanglements in this grim situation had many sordid psychological and social ramifications. (Kim 2004, p.16)

At this time, the doctrine of the Three Ages was widely accepted in Buddhist circles. This distinguished between the Age of Right Law, the Age of Imitative Law and the Age of Degenerate Law. In each case, the law in question was the Dharma, the universal truth. During the first age, it was claimed that the authentic law prevailed. In the second, observance of the Dharma was reduced to little more than going through the motions. The third age was characterised by decay and decline, and it was into this third age that Dōgen was born, although Dōgen himself would subsequently dismiss the classification of the three ages as having any truth or significance as far as the practice of Zen was concerned. In *Bendōwa* (*The Wholehearted Way*) he referred to the issue through a rhetorical question and answer:

> Question Fifteen:
> Can we attain realisation if we practice, even in this last age of decline?
>
> Reply:
> In the scriptural schools they explain various names and aspects, but in the true Mahāyāna teachings dharma is not divided into periods of truth, imitation and decline. Instead, it is taught that everyone attains the way by practice. Particularly in this correctly transmitted teaching of *zazen*, you are enriched with the treasure of yourself, entering dharma and leaving bondage behind. (Tanahashi 1995, p.156)

Bendōwa, however, was written after he had 'completed' his 'life's quest of the great matter' (Tanahashi 1995, p.144) or, as it is more often stated, had 'clarified the great matter' (Uchiyama 1997, p.20), and this brings us to the second reason for Dōgen's feeling of spiritual restlessness. What perplexed him was why it was necessary to practise Zen at all. If, as is affirmed by Buddhist teaching, everything is already endowed with Buddha nature or, to put it another way, all things are enlightened from the beginning, what is the purpose of practice? Since no one was able to answer Dōgen's question to his satisfaction, he decided to leave Japan and travel to China, the country to which Bodhidharma had 'taken' Zen from India at the end of the fifth century CE, in the hope that someone there might be able to help clarify the matter for him.

He left Japan, therefore, in 1223, with his teacher, Myōzen, and a handful of others, and spent four years there, before returning in 1227. Two encounters were of vital significance for him in helping him to resolve the issue with which he was wrestling. Both were with monks, although their roles were very different. The first was a cook and the second an abbot.

Dōgen and the small group travelling with him had set sail from Hakata in Chikuzen in the second month of 1223 and arrived at Ch'ing-yüan-fu in Mingchou in April of that same year. While Myōzen, Dōgen's teacher, was keen to live in a monastic community from the start, Dōgen continued to live on the ship for some three months, 'being unable' – for whatever reason – as he commented, 'to disembark immediately' (Dōgen & Uchiyama 2005, p.10), and it was during this time that he met a 61-year-old Chinese monk, who was the *tenzō* or head cook of the monastery on Mount A-yü-wang. The *tenzō* had come to the ship to buy mushrooms from the Japanese merchants who were on board. The elderly man told Dōgen that he had been a monk for some 40 years, and that although he had lived in several monasteries, he had spent much of his time totally confused about what he was doing.[7] Less than a year before the meeting of the two men, the monk had been appointed *tenzō*, but he was concerned that the day following the conversation he was having with Dōgen was a festival and that he had nothing special to offer the monks.

In the course of the conversation, it transpired that the *Tenzō* had travelled some 14 miles from his temple and was intending to return as soon as he had bought the mushrooms, whereupon Dōgen asked him whether there were not others in such a large monastery who could not do the work for him. The *tenzō* explained that this was *his* work, not that of others, and that, in any case, he had not requested permission to stay away any longer. For Dōgen, this clearly touched something of a raw nerve and brought even further to the surface the question with which he had been wrestling, and which had been the catalyst for his journey to China in the first place. For the vividness of the conversation that followed, it is worth reproducing Dōgen's own account:

> But why, when you are so old, do you do the hard work of a *tenzō*? Why do you not spend your time practising *zazen* or working on the *kōans* of former teachers? Is there something special to be gained from working particularly as a *tenzō*?
>
> He burst out laughing and remarked, 'My good friend from abroad! You do not yet understand what

---

7   In his notes on the translation, Wright suggests that this should be understood as an 'expression of modesty on the part of the monk' (Dōgen & Uchiyama 2005, p.102, n.30).

practice is all about, nor do you know the meaning of the characters'.

When I heard this old monk's words I was taken aback and felt greatly ashamed. So I asked him, 'What are the characters and what is practice?'

He replied, 'If you do not deceive yourself about this problem, you will be a man of the Way'. At the time, I was unable to grasp the meaning of his words. (Dōgen & Uchiyama 2005, p.11)

It is actually rather encouraging to realise that great people like Dōgen are no different from us. He, too, struggled with an inability to see, to 'get it'. In his own mind, *zazen* and other activities – such as cooking – were separate. What he could not yet see was that it was this very separation in his own mind which was the cause of his dissatisfaction and restlessness. So it is somewhat ironic that it was actually an encounter with an abbot, who, by virtue of being wholeheartedly committed to *zazen*, helped him to see what *zazen* really is, which in turn enabled him to overcome the separation in his own mind, thus making all activity – including *zazen* – one.

Not until two years after his arrival in China did Dōgen come across Ju-Ching. Dōgen was actually on the point of returning to Japan in a state of some considerable discontentment. He had spent two years at the Ching-tê-ssŭ temple, but still had not been able to resolve his question. He decided, therefore, to visit a succession of monasteries, but having done so, still remained dissatisfied. A chance meeting with an old monk set him off in the direction of Mount T'ien-t'ung monastery, where Ju-Ching was the abbot.

Ju-Ching clearly had a considerable reputation and was well known for having spurned all worldly fame. The most significant thing about him as far as Dōgen was concerned, though, was that he advocated *shikan-taza* or 'just sitting'. It is important not to misunderstand this. It did not mean that only sitting to the exclusion of ever doing anything else was all that mattered; that would clearly be an absurdity, to say nothing of an impossibility. What it meant was that *zazen* was just *zazen* and nothing else. *Zazen* required that it be conducted without preconceived notions of what it should be or what it should achieve or what benefit it might bring. In other words, all attachments, judgements, thoughts, ideas and concepts had to be released. When you sit *zazen*, just sit *zazen*.

The initial meeting between Dōgen and Ju-Ching was clearly extremely felicitous. Each recognised in the other something special and Ju-Ching took Dōgen under his wing in a very close way. Dōgen resolved to practise *shikan-taza* with all his strength, determination and commitment. Ju-Ching himself practised *shikan-taza* day-in and day-out without fail, and this in itself must have had a considerable impact on Dōgen. Ju-Ching's teaching concerning *shikan-taza* did not fully penetrate Dōgen, however, until, as is so often the case in Zen practice, words said at just the right moment spoke volumes and everything suddenly became clear.

It happened that early one morning in 1225, the monks were sitting *zazen* as they usually did. The monk sitting next to Dōgen, though, had dozed off. This did not escape the hawk-eyed Ju-Ching's notice, who bellowed at him: 'In *zazen* it is imperative to cast off the body and mind. How could you indulge in sleeping?' The effect of this remark was that it 'shook Dōgen's whole being to the core, and then an inexpressible, ecstatic joy engulfed his heart' (Kim 2004, p.36). This was the clarification of the great matter for which Dōgen had long been searching. Exactly what, then, we might well ask, was this clarification?

Dōgen's clarification of the great matter

The words which reverberated through Dōgen's whole being were obviously those concerning the casting off of body and mind. Their impact is evidenced by the fact that in his *Genjō Kōan* (*Actualising the Fundamental Point*) he makes explicit reference to these words:

> To study the Buddha way is to study the self. To study the self is to forget the self. To forget the self is to be actualised by myriad things. When actualised by myriad things, your body and mind as well as the bodies and minds of others drop away. No trace of realisation remains, and this no-trace continues endlessly. (Tanahashi 1995, p.70)

'Study' in this case is not academic study or the study of the self objectively. It really means 'intimacy' or coming to know the self with the self – if that way of putting it does not add to possible confusion. The problem for Dōgen, as it is for us, is that we separate and compartmentalise. This was precisely what troubled Dōgen in his conversation with the *tenzō*. Dōgen assumed that cooking had nothing to do with practice; it was much more important to sit *zazen* and forget other activities. When the *tenzō* remarked that Dōgen did not yet understand what practice was all about, he was indicating that every activity, whatever it may be, has to be approached with the same wholehearted attitude as *zazen*. Then everything becomes practice. Dōgen, however, had to discover that it was the separation in his own mind that prevented him from seeing just this. He had to learn to let go, to allow body and mind to 'drop off' and then see that when he allowed his notion of a separate self to fall away, he awoke to the 'myriad things'. Indeed, enlightenment is waking up to the fact that the myriad things are the self.

The clarification of the great matter that Dōgen found was that he did not need to practise in order to become enlightened. It was rather the case that practice was itself the very manifestation of enlightenment. When body and mind drop off, when the concept of a separate self disappears, there is nothing separate needed to attain enlightenment. Practice and enlightenment are one. In this sense, there is nothing to distinguish between sitting *zazen* and preparing meals in the monastery kitchen. As Dōgen himself put in *Gyōji* (*Continuous Practice*): 'Do not sit and wait for enlightenment, for great enlightenment is to be found in everyday activities such as eating or drinking tea' (Cook 2002, p.144), and in *Kajō* (*Everyday Life*): 'The very best thing is that everything is just eating rice and drinking tea. However, doing *zazen* alone on Ta Hsiung Peak is the same as eating rice and drinking tea' (Cook 2002, p.155). In each case, it is the self functioning as the self.

The issue is the same one that Huike struggled with when he went to Bodhidharma in the hope that he would be able to set his mind at rest. When Bodhidharma sent Huike away to search for his mind, he surely knew that Huike would return to say that he could not find it. Huike discovered that it was the very creation of the idea of a separate self that was itself the problem, and it was this that enabled Huike to awaken. He had tried so hard, yet this effort somehow reinforced the sense of something separate. He needed to let go and awaken to his true nature. Suzuki puts it well:

> So long as you try to find your true nature by practice, you cannot find it. But if you find your true nature in practice, or if you think the practice itself is your true nature, that is enlightenment. Past sages found their true nature in practice. We should find our true nature in the same practice. That is true realisation.
>
> The practice is not some means to attain enlightenment. Before you attain enlightenment, you are just an ordinary person. After you attain enlightenment, you are a sage. That we move ourselves and understand all things is ignorance. When we try to attain enlightenment by practice, we are ignorant. Truth will come by itself, and we will find ourselves in the truth, in the practice. That is enlightenment. (Suzuki 2011, p.108)

Uchiyama puts it in much the same way:

> Since enlightenment is in practice, we have to continue to practise ceaselessly and endlessly. But while you are actually practising, you shouldn't think that 'you' are practising. Though you are practising, you should let go of the thought of practising. Within this letting go, the original reality is actualised; as Dōgen Zenji said, the original enlightenment fills our hands. Right there, the reality of practice is manifested. This is *shikan* (just doing) practice. From the beginning our self is living out reality. But when we just practice, letting go of even such an idea

and casting off original enlightenment, then our practice actualises reality going beyond reality. (Uchiyama 1997, p.173–174)

This is the attitude of mind with which we are to approach sitting and every other aspect of life. There is a temptation, after all, to make 'Zen' just yet another separate activity, whereas Zen is actually the whole of life. It does not always feel like that, though, nor is it always easy. Sometimes we feel, as with Dōgen or Huike, that everything is a very considerable struggle. This is why the desire to clarify the great matter arises within all of us. Each of us has to do this in terms of our own life and not someone else's. We have to take responsibility for our own lives.

Summary: two different journeys to enlightenment

This chapter has sought to explore something of what is involved in taking responsibility for our own lives. Although a creation of the imagination, the character of Parsifal, nevertheless, represents something archetypal in us. His journey from an unawakened to an awakened state is, in one way or another, the one that every human being has to make. Waking up to this truth is the beginning of what it means to begin to take responsibility for our lives. Parsifal himself spent a considerable time in an unawakened state, and yet it was through all the various circumstances of his life that he was gradually woken up, until, finally, his encounter with temptation and suffering led to self-knowledge. As he let go of his egocentricity, the 'original reality was 'actualised', the 'original enlightenment filled his hands' (Uchiyama 1997, p.173–174) and manifested itself as compassion. It was at the moment that he assumed full responsibility for his life.

Dōgen's journey was a rather different one. On the surface, it would seem as if the description 'unawakened' scarcely applied to him. Despite the loss of both parents at a very tender age, Dōgen seems to have shown no signs of any negative *karma* in relation to these two deaths. On the contrary, it was the death of his mother which stiffened his resolve to become a monk, in order to 'seek the truth of Buddhism and strive to relieve the tragic sufferings of humanity' (Kim 2004, p.19). And yet it was not quite so straightforward. Just as Parsifal failed to understand his '*grosse Schuld*' ('*grievous guilt*') (Wagner 1962, p.53) in gratuitously killing the swan, so Dōgen also failed to comprehend what the *tenzō* was getting at: 'My good friend from abroad! You do not yet understand what practice is all about, nor do you know the meaning of the characters' (Dōgen & Uchiyama 2005, p.11).

It might be suggested, though, that these two scenarios are wholly different from one another. Failing to understand one's guilt for killing a swan is of a completely different order from failing to comprehend the nature of practising Zen. In many ways, this is precisely the point, though, for taking responsibility for one's own life involves accepting all the different karmic effects that have contributed to our lives being as they are at this moment, and that necessarily involves appreciating that *karma* works itself out in one way for this person, and another for that. The lives of the fictional Parsifal and the historical Dōgen are different. And yet, for all the dissimilarities, the end result is the same. Each are led by a path that enables them to realise enlightenment. As Schofield notes: 'The quest of the Holy Grail is the quest for enlightenment, and the attainment of the quest of the Holy Grail is the attainment of enlightenment and salvation' (Schofield 2007, p.33), just as for Dōgen the urgent need to 'clarify the great matter', as to whether one needed to practise in order to attain enlightenment, was resolved once he saw that practice was itself the very manifestation of enlightenment. The point is that the life for which each took responsibility was different, but precisely by virtue of taking responsibility for their own particular lives, they were led to the same discovery that all lives are essentially one, that we are not separate. The consequence of taking responsibility for our own lives is the realisation of the oneness of all life.

Chapter 4

The Great Death

Life and death

With reference to the fictional life of Parsifal and the historical life of Zen Master Dōgen, the previous chapter explored something of what is involved in taking responsibility for one's life. What about death, though? Where does death fit in and what is the relationship between life and death? Whatever else might be said about life, death is an absolute fact. It is inevitable, unavoidable and non-negotiable, and it colours the whole of life. The process of coming to terms with death in Zen is often referred to as 'clarifying the great matter of life and death'. In this context, Zen speaks, too, of the 'Great Death'. What is this and what light might it show on the death of Jesus?

In this chapter, I shall explore the mysterious and ambiguous relationship between life and death by reflecting on some aspects of Jesus' life and teaching, which will lead into further engagement with some *kōans*, before returning at the end to consider the significance of Jesus' own death. We begin, though, with the moving story of Kisa Gotami.

The story of Kisa Gotami

In the *Discourses of the Ancient Nuns*, the story is told of how Bikkhuni Gotami, one of Shakyamuni Buddha's monastic followers, was out begging for her day's food, as was the custom of Buddhist monastics at the time. Having been given all that she needed, she sat down under a tree to meditate. No sooner had she begun, than she was distracted by Mara, the Evil One:

> Why now, when your son is dead,
> Do you sit alone with tearful face?
> Having entered the woods all alone,
> Are you on the lookout for a man?

Initially, she was perplexed, wondering who this was who was addressing her, but once she had identified who it was, she replied:

> I've gotten past the death of sons;
> With this, the search for men has ended.
> I do not sorrow, I do not weep,
> Nor do I fear you, friend.

> Delight everywhere has been destroyed,
> The mass of darkness has been sundered.
> Having conquered the army of Death,
> I dwell without defiling taints.[1]

---

1   Bodhi (1997) Section 3, 'Gotami'.

There is a yet another story behind these rather enigmatic words, without which it is difficult to appreciate fully what they are getting at, and it goes something like this.

Kisa Gotami was a young woman from a wealthy family, happily married to a well-to-do merchant. When she gave birth to her first child, a boy, she was delighted, but when he was little more than 12 months old, he fell ill and died suddenly. Unsurprisingly, Kisa Gotami was utterly distraught and nearly driven her out of her mind with grief. In a state of utter dejection and in a permanent state of tears, she carried her dead son in her arms and went from house to house, begging all the people in the town to tell her of a way to bring him back to life.

Nobody could help her, but Kisa Gotami would not give up. Finally, she came across one of the Buddha's followers, who advised her to go and see the Buddha himself.

When she carried the dead child to the Buddha and told him her sad story, he listened with immense patience and compassion, and then said to her, 'Kisa Gotami, there is only one way to solve your problem. Go and find me four or five mustard seeds from any family in which there has never been a death'.

Filled with hope at last, Kisa Gotami set off straightaway to find such a household. Very soon, however, she discovered that every family she visited had experienced the death of one person or another. Then the penny dropped. She understood what the Buddha had wanted her to find out for herself – that suffering is a part of life, and death comes to us all. Once Kisa Gotami accepted the fact that death is inevitable, she was able to stop grieving. She took the child's body away and later returned to the Buddha to become one of his followers.[2]

This is an extraordinarily touching and very human story. Although it is not everyone who is unfortunate enough to have to go through all that is involved in losing a child, the experience of loss is self-evidently universal. We all experience death, including our own and that of others. Where our own deaths are concerned, we spend a great deal of time and energy trying to avoid the inevitable. The younger we are, the less inclined we are to face our own mortality. Often it is the death of a contemporary in their childhood, teenage years or early twenties that brings us up short. It does not necessarily follow, though, that advancing in age automatically brings with it an increase of wisdom in this particular regard. Western culture as a whole, for example, seems to be much less accepting of the fact of death than Eastern cultures are. Even among those who do not espouse belief in immortality of any kind, life can often be characterised by an urgent and desperate need to secure a name for themselves that will endure, or to secure a legacy of some kind.

Kisa Gotami's encounter with Mara, as quoted above, comes in the form of a temptation to perpetuate her bloodline. Mara assumes that the only possible way for Kisa Gotami to deal with the loss of her son is to have another one. 'Are you on the lookout for a man?' In other words, 'Are you in search of a suitable mate to help you conceive another child?' Mara is misguided in two respects.

---

2   This story is not to be found in any of the Buddhist scriptures but has simply been circulated in oral tradition. A version of it can be accessed online at www.buddhanet.net/e-learning/buddhism/bs-s03a.htm.

First, he implies, crassly and insensitively, that the love that Kisa Gotami has for her son is not particular and uniquely valuable, that she could deal with the loss of one son simply by replacing him with another. Second, he intimates that the pain of death and loss can be averted by going on giving birth. What would happen when that was no longer possible, though, and Kisa Gotami had gone past the age of conceiving and bearing children? Suppose, as is sometimes – heartbreakingly – the case, that a woman suffers a succession of miscarriages and is unable to carry children in the womb to full term, or that parents lose all their children as a result of illness, accident or war. What then? What more can be done to avoid the fact of death? Kisa Gotami has clearly worked this all out and realised that death, pain and loss are inevitable components of life, so she replies that she has come to terms with the death of her son and, therefore, no longer has the need of a man to ensure continuity and assuage her pain. At this decisive point, Mara disappears.

Accepting the fact of death and coming to terms with it is a lifelong task with which most of us struggle. However much the story of Kisa Gotami makes sense in our heads, it is much harder to find a place for it in our hearts. It simply seems to go against the grain of things. And yet Christianity and Zen invite us to look death in the eye as an unavoidable fact and, in so doing, discover that life and death are mysteriously intertwined, that living inescapably involves dying, that if we wish truly to live, we must also learn to die.

The mysterious ambiguity of life and death

In their different ways, Jesus and Shakyamuni Buddha each had to resolve or clarify for themselves 'the great matter of life and death'. The historically distinctive thing about the Christian faith is that it has at its centre a most gruesome death by crucifixion – and also a resurrection. While Shakyamuni Buddha died peacefully in old age, Jesus had to endure death on the public stage when he was little more than 30 years of age. Right up until the night before his death, he was wrestling with the meaning of his own death, and whether it was right that he should submit to it in the manner in which it was being presented to him. All four gospels record that Jesus was arrested in a garden – or, in Luke's case, a 'place' on the Mount of Olives, and John does not actually name it as Gethsemane (Matthew 26.36ff; Mark 14.32ff; Luke 22.39ff and John 18.1ff) – and, with the exception of John, they each show how the imminence of death put Jesus under extreme pressure. Luke's gospel portrays how 'in his anguish he prayed more earnestly, and his sweat became like great drops of blood falling down on the ground' (Luke 22.44). It was only his surrender to the Father that enabled him to accept what lay before him as the very outcome and meaning of his life: 'Father, if you are willing, remove this cup from me; yet, not my will but yours be done' (Luke 22.42).

Crucifixion is just about the most brutal form of execution ever devised, and in many ways it is a matter of some wonder that the preaching of the gospel, with such a death uncomfortably at the heart of its message, was ever able to connect with people and become established in their hearts and minds. Perhaps it was, in part, its sheer unlikelihood, incredibility and incomprehensibility that enabled it to cut through people's misgivings. It is scarcely surprising that the apostle Paul marvelled at it, too:

> For Jews demand signs and Greeks desire wisdom, but we proclaim Christ crucified, a stumbling-block to Jews and foolishness to Gentiles, but to those who are the called, both Jews and Gentiles, Christ the power of God and the wisdom of God. For God's foolishness is wiser than human wisdom, and God's weakness is stronger than human strength. (1 Corinthians 1.22–25)

The Christian faith is not only about death, though; it is also – and just as much – about life. Although in the temporal sense, it invites us to see life and death in linear terms, with resurrection following death, it is perhaps not so simple and straightforward as we might think. When Jesus is portrayed in the gospels as calling people to follow him, his disciples respond without a moment's thought, and yet, as the story unfolds, it becomes clear that not only is Jesus' own path towards crucifixion, so, in one way or another, is that of his followers. I have often wondered what would happen if the Church today sought to communicate its message to those unfamiliar with it by saying something like: 'Come and die'. Such a strategy would almost certainly be resisted on the grounds that it was likely to meet with little success, and yet it would surely be authentic. It would also be quite true to the gospel, though, to adopt the opposite approach: 'Come and live'. After all, in the Gospel of John, Jesus says: 'The thief comes only to steal and kill and destroy. I came that they might have life, and have it abundantly'

(John 10.10). Following Jesus is about both discovering life and also embracing death.

Life and death are inextricably bound up with one another. When Jesus says, 'Very truly, I tell you, unless a grain of wheat falls into the earth and dies, it remains just a single grain; but if it dies, it bears much fruit', he is, of course, speaking of his own imminent death. As he continues, though, it is clear that he is referring to his followers as well, 'Those who love their life lose it, and those who hate their life in this world will keep it for eternal life. Whoever serves me must follow me, and where I am, my servant will be also. Whoever serves me, the Father will honour' (John 12.24–26). The eternal life – *zoē aiōnios* – to which Jesus refers, is not predominantly some future existence, it really means the *reality and quality of God's life experienced now*. Living in the full awareness of and receptiveness to this divine life now, though, does not anaesthetise us to the reality of suffering, loss and death: it actually heightens it, but in such a way that they are accepted as part of what life is, and thus it liberates.

This is partly what is suggested when, after his resurrection, Jesus is seen still to be bearing the marks and wounds of the crucifixion. Thomas, for example, having been absent when the Risen Christ appeared to the other disciples, declared that he would not believe what they had told him unless he was able to see the mark of the nails in his hands and of the spear in his side. A week later, the Risen Christ appeared and invited Thomas to do just that (John 20.24–27). The wounds of suffering and death were imprinted in the risen body. In the same way, the Church understands that the Christ who is 'taken up' into heaven at the Ascension, is the one in whom the whole of creation is taken up and enabled to share in the fullness of divine life. The Ascended Christ, however, is also the Risen Christ, the one who still bears the same marks and wounds of the crucifixion. The phrase, 'in the midst of life we are in death', is apposite here, but it could just as easily be turned around to say, 'in the midst of death we are in life'.[3]

Something of this apparent ambiguity is caught by T.S. Eliot in his poem, *Journey of the Magi*. Eliot's concern seems to be to turn his back on much of the superficiality of the sentimental approaches to the birth of Christ and get under the skin of what the journey might actually have been like for the wise men. Just as most people are grief-stricken at the death of a child, so, too, are most overjoyed at the birth. Although the wise men are travelling to find and celebrate a birth, Eliot has them ask whether the purpose of the journey was actually for a birth or a death:

> …were we led all that way for
> Birth or Death? There was a birth, certainly,
> We had evidence and no doubt. I had seen birth and death,
> But had thought they were different; this Birth was
> Hard and bitter agony for us, like Death, our death.
> We returned to our places, these Kingdoms,

---

3   The Latin phrase, *Media vita in morte sumus*, is the first part of an antiphon attributed to the Benedictine monk, Notker the Stammerer (c.840–912), but is actually thought to have originated in France sometime around 750. The *York Breviary* makes provision for it to be sung as an antiphon at Compline on the fourth Sunday of Lent, while in the *Sarum Breviary* it is to be sung from the third to the fifth Sunday of Lent. Archbishop Thomas Cranmer incorporated the English translation of it, 'In the midst of life we are in death', into the *Book of Common Prayer*.

But no longer at ease here, in the old dispensation,
With an alien people clutching their gods.
I should be glad of another death. (Eliot 2004, p.104)

In this poem, Eliot wonderfully captures the mysterious ambiguity of life and death. The journey itself of the wise men involves a death of some kind, leaving behind an old way of life, the 'old dispensation', so the birth of Christ brought with it death of a kind. What is the death referred to in the final line, though? The death of the wise men, or of Christ, or both?

Sometimes it is not actually possible be sure which is which as far as life and death are concerned. The members of the church in Sardis, for example, are reprimanded in the Revelation to John: 'I know your works; you have a name for being alive, but you are dead. Wake up, and strengthen what remains and is at the point of death, for I have not found your works perfect in the sight of my God' (Revelation 3.1b–2). What appears to be life might actually be death and *vice versa*. This requires of us that we resist making quick judgements about what does appear to be life or death in a dualistic way, for such judgements can result in our missing the mark completely. Zen revels in such ambiguity, but not for the sake of trivial amusement. In so doing, it invites us to ponder really profound questions about life and death. In the final analysis, clarifying the great matter has to do with clarifying the 'great matter of life and death', so let us explore this in relation to several *kōans* and then see what light this might shed on our understanding of the life and death of Christ – and, of course, our own. The first is entitled, *Tao Wu's Condolence Call*, and is Case 55 from *The Blue Cliff Record*.

Tao Wu's Condolence Call

Tao Wu and Chien Yuan went to a house to make a condolence call. Yuan hit the coffin and said, 'Alive or dead?' Wu said, 'I won't say alive, and I won't say dead.' Yuan said, 'Why won't you say?' Wu said, 'I won't say.' Halfway back, as they were returning, Yuan said, 'Tell me right away, Teacher; if you don't tell me, I'll hit you.' Wu said, 'You may hit me, but I won't say.' Yuan then hit him. Later Tao Wu passed on. Yuan went to Shih Shuang and brought up the foregoing story. Shuang said, 'I won't say alive, and I won't say dead.' Yuan said, 'Why won't you say?' Shuang said, 'I won't say, I won't say.' At these words, Yuan had an insight. One day Yuan took a hoe into the teaching hall and crossed back and forth, from east to west and west to east. Shuang said, 'What are you doing?' Yuan said, 'I'm looking for relics of our late master.' Shuang said, 'Vast waves spread far and wide, foaming billows flood the skies – what relics of our late master are you looking for?' Hsueh Tau added a comment saying, 'Heavens! Heavens!' Yuan said, 'This is just where I should apply effort.' Fu of T'ai Yuan said, 'The late master's relics are still present.'

On the face of it, this looks like an extraordinarily insensitive pastoral visit. Behind Yuan's question, though, perhaps we can hear an urgent, even desperate, question. However much we might think that we have sorted out what we believe about life and death, particularly about what happens after death, being confronted with the sheer concrete reality of death can raise such questions for us over and over again. Seeing the body in the coffin appears to have done just this for Yuan. There is a kind of burning intensity of doubt behind Yuan's question that suggests that what he had thought up to this point no longer sufficed.

There is something very similar here to the first *kōan* Zen students sit with, the first case of *The Gateless Gate*, known as *Jōshū's Dog*. It is very short and to the point:

Jōshū's Dog

A monk asked Jōshū in all earnestness, 'Does a dog have Buddha nature or not?'

Jōshū said, 'Mu!' (Yamada 2004, p.11)

It should be noted that the monk asks the question in all earnestness; this is a serious question for him, a question, as it were, of life and death. The odd thing, however, is that the monk would certainly have been taught that all beings are endowed with Buddha nature, including dogs. So what prompted his question? Let us assume that the monk might have caught sight of a dog, thin and emaciated, perhaps, which made him say to himself, 'I know that all beings are endowed with Buddha nature, even dogs, but *this* dog?' A doubt had been raised in his mind and he found, perhaps, that this doubt haunted him day and night. It might even have caused him sleepless nights.

Does this sort of question not arise for us in all sorts of circumstances? It is firmly embedded in Christian understanding, for example, that all people, whatever their background, situation, appearance, race, gender, belief or lifestyle, are created in the image and likeness of God. This is what is affirmed in the book of Genesis when human beings are created, before anything else actually happens (Genesis 1.26–27). Is it not the case, though, that particular people on certain occasions cause us to question this? Hitler? Stalin? The murderer? The child abuser? The rapist? The list could go on endlessly. However much we might believe it in our heads to be true, we actually set limits. The belief is abstract but the actual person is particular, and it is the particular that raises doubts and questions for us.

This seems to have been the case with the monk. He knew in principle that all beings are endowed with Buddha nature, but this particular dog caused him to wonder. If, however, he was having second thoughts about a dog, where would that chain of thought end? What about himself? Was he really endowed with Buddha nature? Are there really no limits? Is the line not be drawn somewhere? Such doubt would have unsettled him, quite seriously, it would seem. So he went to the one person who could reassure him with a definitive answer: Jōshū. Jōshū's response, though, was of no immediate help at all: 'Mu!' 'Mu' really means 'no', 'not' or 'nothing', so what was Jōshū getting at? What kind of an answer was that? It can only have intensified the monk's inner turmoil, for if 'Mu' was taken to mean 'no', then this would have conflicted directly with the teaching of the Buddha. The monk, therefore, was placed in an even greater quandary than before he asked the question. Jōshū was well aware, however, that whatever he might have said to confirm what the monk had been taught would and could only have given temporary satisfaction and relief. In the end, no one else could resolve the matter for the monk. He alone had to resolve it for himself. He did that, as have countless students throughout the centuries, by sitting with 'Mu', wrestling with it, following Mumon's advice to:

concentrate your whole self into this Mu, making your whole body with its 360 bones and joints and 84,000 pores into a solid lump of doubt. Day and night, without ceasing, keep digging into it, but don't take it as 'nothingness' or as 'being' or 'non-being'. It must be like a red-hot iron ball which you have gulped down and which you try to vomit up but cannot. You must extinguish all delusive thoughts and beliefs which you have cherished up to the present. After a certain period of such efforts, Mu will come to fruition, and inside and out will become one naturally. You will then be like a dumb man who has had a dream. You will know yourself and for yourself only.

Then all of a sudden, Mu will break open. It will astonish the heavens and shake the earth... Though you may stand on the brink of life and death, you will enjoy the great freedom...you will live in the Samadhi of innocent play. (Yamada 2004, pp.11–12)

What we discover, as did the monk – presumably – by sitting with 'Mu', is that the matter is resolved not by resisting our doubt, anxiety and insecurity, but by becoming one with it, by finding that no abstract answer will finally satisfy us. When we become one with 'Mu', the internal division between us and our thoughts comes tumbling down, and we experience for ourselves what 'Mu' is.

When Yuan went with Wu to make their condolence call, the sight of the dead body must have had the same sort of effect on Yuan as did the dog on the monk in *Jōshū's Dog*. Whatever rational position Yuan had reached about death up to this point suddenly collapsed. This is not really at all surprising, though; it happens to all of us. When someone close to us dies, we might well start wondering about the present status of that person. Is that it or are they still alive in some sense? If so, where and in what way? More often than not, though, it is the way the death of someone else impinges on *us* that is more significant. What will happen to *me* when I die? What will *my* death be like? How will *I* cope with pain? Reactions can be tinged with more than a hint of selfishness, too. On seeing or hearing of a ghastly road, rail, air or sea accident, we might catch ourselves being pleased that we were not involved in it. We have our lives, even if they do not. Death, after all, is for other people.

Yuan was faced with the prospect of his own death as he stood looking at the coffin, and his insistent question, 'Alive or dead?' was surely a deeply personal one. The corpse brought him face to face with his own mortality. What did he think about death? This question, however, must have made him think just as much about life: What are life and death? What is it all about? What happens to *me* when *I* die? Is there a 'me' anyway?

These are very human questions and the great faith traditions suggest a variety of possible answers. Such answers only go so far, though. They are all right in the abstract, but what happens in the face of the concrete reality of our own deaths? We might wish to die a 'good death', and we can make all sorts of plans for how we will die. Circumstances might well overtake us, though, and our plans can fly out of the window. The stories and scenarios which we conceive in our imaginations concerning our own deaths, or the deaths of others, fail to stand up to the reality of what actually happens. In which case, in what way can I prepare for my own death?

Part of the answer to that question is to be found in the way we live our lives. Life itself very rarely turns out to be exactly what we think, hope or would like it to be. It simply flows in and of itself, rather like a river finding its own way across all sorts of terrain. Indeed, many of the difficulties we encounter in life arise because of our attempts to make our lives go in the way we think they should or want them to, rather than just letting life be. And life inescapably includes death. In fact, it is not always clear what is actually life and what is death.

To put it another way, loss is an integral part of our everyday experience. Nor is this something regrettable or to be avoided. Very often, life can only flow if we let go of it. Take the development of a child, for example. A baby can only live if it loses the security and safety of the womb. Birth is a precarious business, though less so now than in the past, certainly in some, if not all countries. Birth, however, involves, even requires, a death of a kind. Without the death of the symbiotic relationship of mother and child, life in this world would not be possible.

So, too, as the child learns, grows and develops, it has to die to all kinds of securities. The temporary absence of a parent, for example, even if they are only in the next room, can cause distress early on in a baby's life, but it has to learn to tolerate such things, if it is gradually to stand on its own two feet. Little by little, it trusts, on the basis of experience, if it is fortunate, that the parent will indeed return, and thus begins to tolerate longer periods of absence without undue anxiety. On the basis of this security, the child itself begins to develop an adventurous approach to the world, exploring all sorts of things without fear, something which causes more anxiety on the part of parents than the child itself. This reaches a significant milestone when a child is first cared for by a childminder or starts at nursery or school, and temporarily 'loses' or 'dies' to the security of the parent–child relationship in order to 'come alive' to other possibilities in life, without which they would not grow. This pattern continues throughout our lives, such that 'life' only seems to be possible if 'death' is accepted as part and parcel of it. It is this, in part, which enables us to face our own physical deaths with the same trust with which we approach life as a whole. Just as birth in the first place requires us to die to life in the womb, so death can be seen as the birth of a new adventure.

In the same way that Jōshū refused to answer the monk's own question for him in the way he wanted, neither did Wu – or Shuang in his turn for that matter – give Yuan the answer he thought he was looking for: 'I won't say alive and I won't say dead.' In one sense, this seems entirely counter-intuitive. Of course the person is dead! Here is the lifeless corpse lying in front of our eyes. What is death, though? What is life? Is it either this or that? Is death one thing and life another? Wu and Shuang alike did Yuan the great service of not offering a pat answer but, instead, directed Yuan to his own experience. What did his own concrete experience of life and death tell him? 'You will know yourself and for yourself only.'

Zen speaks not only about clarifying the great matter of life and death but also of the 'Great Death'. To explore just what this is about, it will be helpful to turn to another *kōan*, Case 23 from *The Gateless Gate*.

Think No Good Nor Evil

The case

The sixth patriarch was once pursued by the monk Myō as far as Mount Daiyu. The patriarch, seeing Myō coming, laid the robe and bowl on a rock and said, 'This robe represents the faith. How can it be competed for by force? I will allow you to take it away.'

Myō tried to lift it up, but it was as immovable as a mountain. Terrified and trembling with awe, he said, 'I came for the Dharma, not the robe. I beg you, lay brother, please reveal it to me.'

The patriarch said: '[At the very moment you were chasing after me] without thinking good or evil, what was the primal face of Monk Myō?' In that instant, Myō suddenly attained deep realisation, and his whole body was covered with sweat. In tears, he bowed and said, 'Besides the secret words and secret meaning you have just revealed to me, is there anything else deeper yet?'

The patriarch said, 'What I have now preached to you is no secret at all. If you reflect on your own true face, the secret will be found within yourself.'

Myō said, 'Though I have been at Ōbai with the other monks, I have never realised what my true self is. Now, thanks to your instruction, I know it is like a man who drinks water and knows for himself whether it is cold or warm. Now you, lay brother, are my master.' The patriarch said, 'If that is the way you feel, let us both have Ōbai for our master. Be mindful and hold fast to what you have realised.'

Mumon's commentary

It should be said of the sixth patriarch that his action sprang from urgent circumstances. His kindness is like that of a grandmother who peels a fresh litchi, removes the seed, and puts it into your mouth so that all you have to do is swallow it.

The verse

It can't be described! It can't be pictured!
It can't be sufficiently praised! Stop trying to grasp it with your head!
There is nowhere to hide the primal face;
Even when the world is destroyed, it is indestructible.

As was the case with *Bodhidharma Puts the Mind to Rest* in Chapter 2, a little background information is required to help see what the *kōan* is getting at.[4]

Background to the *kōan*

The patriarch in question is Eno, otherwise known as Huineng (638–713). His father had died when he was very young and, as a result, he had lived in poverty, while he and his mother tried to support themselves. Being illiterate, all he could do was eke out a meagre living by selling firewood. One day, as he was on his way home from the market where he was selling his wares, he heard someone, probably a monk, chanting the *Diamond Sūtra*, the teaching *par excellence* in Zen concerning emptiness.

---

4   For sources, see Abels (2012, pp.21–33), Ferguson (2011, pp.43–46), and Gu (2016, pp.209–213).

At the words 'non-abiding, mind arising', he had a deep insight. When he asked the person chanting what it was, and was told, he enquired as to where he could find more teaching on the text. When he discovered that the person had obtained his copy from the great Master Hongren, who lived far away in the north, as opposed to the south where Huineng was, he was dismayed. He desperately wanted to study with Hongren, but he also wanted to take care of his mother. Someone apparently gave him the money he needed to provide for his mother, though, and so he set off to visit Hongren at Mount Huangmei, a journey that took him 30 days to complete.

On his arrival, Hongren asked where he had come from. When Huineng told him that he was from the south, a part of the country decidedly lacking in prosperity, Hongren assumed that he was unsophisticated and unintelligent. Illiterate he may have been, but stupid most definitely not. When Huineng responded that as far as Buddha Nature was concerned, there was no north or south, Hongren realised that someone remarkable was standing before him. He invited him to study with him, but, aware that there was much jealousy and competition among the monks in the monastery, suggested that Huineng work in the kitchen and keep a low profile.

One day, Huineng announced that it was his intention to retire, and so he invited the monks to demonstrate their realisation. The Head Monk did so by writing a poem. Hongren praised it, but it was clear that he did not think the monk was fully awake yet. On hearing someone recite the verse, Huineng asked who had written it, and then came up with his own. Being illiterate, he asked someone else to write it on the wall next to the Head Monk's. When Hongren read it, he knew that Huineng was to be his successor. Realising that Huineng's life itself might be at risk if he were to make a public show of it, he entrusted him in private with his master's robe and bowl as a sign of transmission, and then instructed Huineng to leave the monastery and go into hiding. As Huineng was unfamiliar with the northern part of the country, Hongren himself escorted him for part of the journey to ensure that he proceeded in the right direction. Having returned, Hongren did not give any teaching in the monastery for three days, which caused the monks to ask if something was wrong. When Hongren declared that he was old and that he had already passed the teaching down, the community was sent into a frenzy, wondering who on earth his successor could be. Hongren simply said that the teaching had been passed down to the one who was capable. At that, it became clear immediately that it could be none other than Huineng. It is at this point that the *kōan* begins.

Back to the *kōan*

Given that Zen is grounded entirely in personal experience and realisation of enlightenment, it might seem rather strange that there was competition to be Hongren's successor. On reflection, though, it is abundantly clear in all sorts of circumstances that self-centredness and self-seeking can cloud our motives. This was the case with Myō, otherwise known as Huiming. Before becoming a monk, he had been a four-star general in the Chinese army, and, it would appear, someone who was prepared to fight for what he wanted. It was for this reason that he took up the chase after Huineng, in order to wrest from him the outward signs of Dharma transmission, in the hope of snatching Hongren's authority from Huineng.

In the encounter that follows, we can sense the humility not only of Huineng, a characteristic which must have been one of the reasons why Hongren discerned in Huineng someone capable of wisdom, but also the humility of Huiming, who was prepared to surrender himself to Huineng, when he perceived the latter's true realisation. Not wanting to put up any resistance, Huineng set the robe and bowl before Huiming, inviting him to take them, but adding the rider that the Dharma is incapable of being taken by force. This is the significance of the fact that, symbolically, Huiming could not lift the robe and bowl up. In other words, they could not be grasped at selfishly. The Dharma can only be received in an open-handed way. To do that, we have to open ourselves up and let go.

In a lightning flash, Huiming perceived what he really wanted: the truth, which he could only realise for himself personally, rather than the outward signs and trappings of transmission, which, without personal realisation, were worthless: 'I came for the Dharma, not the robe. I beg you, lay brother, please reveal it to me.' In all humility, the former four-star general asked the illiterate kitchen assistant to be his teacher.

How do you teach someone to realise the truth for themselves? Precisely not by cramming people's heads with knowledge to be regurgitated second-hand, or by providing our own answers to other people's deeply personal questions concerning life and death, as if our own answers will do for other people. For all that there are commonalities, no two people's life experiences are identical. We enter into the truth by taking seriously and embracing the totality of our life experience, whatever particular shape it might take. The teacher, and especially the Zen teacher, can do little more than act as a midwife, enabling realisation to come to birth, as it were, of its own accord. Our Buddha nature, our true self, is not something to be added on to who we are, or to be achieved or gained. It is there from the beginning, and it can only be *realised*.

Huineng, then, brings Huiming to the place where he is open to the truth for himself in the context of his own life experience. As a general in the army, he had presumably persuaded himself that in any conflict he was morally aligned with good rather than evil. Perhaps he saw life in black and white terms and was rather rigid in his approach. He was also most likely to have been used to getting his own way. He was, after all, someone to be obeyed rather to obey. As he stood before Huineng, all of this must have seemed to have been to no avail. In that moment, he saw that whatever other goals he had pursued in life, what he really wanted right now was his own personal realisation of the truth of the Dharma. He wanted to realise his true self. He knew that nothing else mattered. He could have the robe and the bowl, but they would not have satisfied him one bit. So Huineng asked him, 'At the very moment of chasing after me, without thinking good or evil, what was the primal face of the monk Myō?' In other words, when you let go of all the habitual judgements and discriminations of the mind, when you stop chasing after what you think you want and need, when you stop asserting your *self*, and stop believing the stories you tell about yourself, and just become still, who are you? In that moment, a space, an empty space, opened up and the scales fell from Huiming's eyes. His true self revealed itself. He knew it first-hand.

He tasted water and knew for himself whether it was cold or warm.

What is it that we awaken to when our 'self' disappears? Not a vacuum or a vacancy but life in all its fullness. It can't be described or pictured, as the verse states. The primal face cannot be hidden, so stop trying to grasp it! As Dōgen says:

> To study the Buddha way is to study the self. To study the self is to forget the self. To forget the self is to be actualised by myriad things. When actualised by myriad things, your body and mind as well as the bodies and minds of others drop away. No trace of realisation remains, and this no-trace continues endlessly. (Tanahashi 1995, p.70)

Huiming awoke to emptiness and discovered, as Dōgen was later to articulate, that when the self disappears, everything is the self, actualised by the myriad things. Emptiness is also oneness, in which there is no separation. Everything is interconnected.

The question to be asked about Huiming, then, is similar to that asked in Eliot's *Journey of the Magi*: is this *kōan* about life or death? The answer, surely, is both. In Zen, Huiming's experience is referred to as the 'Great Death', but 'Great Death' is simultaneously the revelation of 'Great Life'. Huiming 'dies', but in so doing, wakes up and knows the joy and fullness of life. In dying to self we, like him, awaken to self, or, in the words of Shunryu Suzuki, to 'original mind', 'beginner's mind' or 'big mind' (Suzuki 1999, pp.21, 35, 92). This self, however, is always present, never absent, and in it 'everything is included' (Suzuki 1999, p.35); it is who we truly are.

Jōshū asks about death

This brings us, briefly, to a final *kōan*, which takes us on a little further from the stage reached in the previous one. Once again it concerns Jōshū, and, like *Jōshū's Dog*, the case itself is short and to the point:

> Attention! Master Jōshū asked Master Toshi, 'When a man who dies the Great Death revives, what then?' Toshi replied, 'Going by night isn't permitted. You'd better arrive during the day.' (Cleary & Cleary 2013, p.249; Wick 2005, p.196)

It is not my intention to spend much time on this *kōan*, other than to draw attention to the central point. Again, some background information will be helpful, which Wick (2005) provides. Jōshū had heard of Master Toshi's reputation and was on a pilgrimage to where he lived, in the hope of deepening his understanding. As he was on his way, he thought he recognised Toshi and asked him whether he was indeed Toshi. It was Toshi, of course, but Toshi played the innocent and pretended to be a beggar, whereupon Jōshū ignored him and continued on his journey. On his arrival at Toshi's hut, Jōshū entered and sat down. Eventually, Toshi returned carrying a jug of oil. Jōshū remarked that he had heard of Toshi, but that all he had seen since his arrival was an 'old-timer selling oil' (Wick 2005, p.197). Toshi remonstrated with Jōshū that he had seen the old-timer selling oil but that he had not yet recognised the true Toshi. When Jōshū asked who the real Toshi was, Toshi simply lifted up the jug and said, 'Oil, oil!'

The point about this is that dying the Great Death and realising emptiness is at one and the same time giving birth to the Great Life, in what Zen refers to as 'form'. The *Heart Sūtra* declares: 'Form does not differ from emptiness, emptiness does not differ from form. That which is form is emptiness, that which is emptiness form.' In the *kōan*, emptiness is equated with night, and form with day. Emptiness and form, the absolute and the relative, are not be understood dualistically, though; they are neither simply one nor two. Toshi reveals his true self in the very ordinariness of life, in such activities as selling oil. The Great Death does not remove us from life but enables us to enter into it and live it even more fully. Toshi has nothing to prove. He just gets on with his life, however ordinary and humdrum it may seem.

The reflections on these *kōans* have had the purpose of showing how, from the perspective of Zen practice, life and death are found to be mysteriously interwoven. Most of us recoil from death, but, as we have seen, without death there is no real life. In the remaining part of this chapter, I want to look at the death of Jesus and explore what light might be thrown on it by Zen. In particular, I want to suggest that in the way he embraced and underwent the Great Death on the cross, Jesus manifested the 'self' or 'original mind' or 'big mind', precisely because he did not flinch from death and the suffering it entailed, but included it as part of his life. In so doing, he invites us to follow him through the Great Death and discover it to be the gateway to Great Life. In order to see how this might be, we need to begin with the circumstances that led to his death.

The volatile circumstances of Jesus' life

Jesus was born into a political and religious maelstrom. Despite believing that they were loved and chosen by God for the purpose of embodying and revealing the life and character of God for the benefit of the whole world, his people had been continuously subjected to one tragedy, disaster and disappointment after another. Early on in their history they had been taken into slavery in Egypt. Many years later, in the eighth century BCE, the Assyrians had attacked and besieged the northern kingdom of Israel, and then, for most of the sixth century BCE, Israel had had to endure the relentless aggression of the Babylonians, who not only deported vast swathes of the population into exile in Babylon, but also destroyed the things that were the most precious and visible symbols of their identity: the temple and the king's palace.

Although Cyrus of Persia had made it possible for the exiles to return towards the end of the century, the country had subsequently found itself first at the mercy of the Greeks, and then in 63 BCE, the Romans had conquered Jerusalem and subjected the Jewish kingdom to their rule and authority. Throughout almost their entire history, the Jewish people had experienced insecurity, powerlessness and suffering on a colossal scale. It is not surprising, therefore, that many longed for the time when the situation would be redressed, and they would finally be established in peace and security, confident in who they were as the chosen people, and able to live in freedom and prosperity. Jesus was born into a situation where hopes were high and antennae were alert to detect anyone who might look like a possible saviour. Anyone who promised to overthrow the Romans and restore the kingdom of Israel to its rightful place in the world would inevitably be hailed and welcomed as a hero.

In such a volatile situation, anyone who looked like a saviour would have been the recipient of all sorts of expectations and projections. People would have developed their own narratives concerning how everything would be set right, what kind of a person might bring that about, and what life would be like thereafter. Such political programmes, however, were inevitably predicated on assumptions about who were friends and enemies, who was 'one of us' and who was 'one of them'. Wrongs would be avenged and tables turned. Salvation would be exclusive.

When Jesus began to preach that the time had come and that the kingdom of God was near, some, perhaps many, would have begun to wonder whether this was not exactly what they had been waiting for during all those centuries. Not only were there political expectations, though; there were also religious ones. Jews and Gentiles were separate, as was made clear by the way the temple was constructed. There were rules to be kept to ensure ritual purity. Sickness and disease were thought to be in a causal relationship with sin, and contact with death resulted in uncleanness. At the heart of this was the sacrificial system of the Temple, administered by the religious class of priests and Levites, supported by the teaching and interpretation of the *Torah*, the Law, at the hands of rabbis and scribes. The underlying purpose of this whole set-up was to make it possible for people to maintain relationship with and find favour with God.

Approval of Jesus begins to turn sour

When Jesus began his public ministry, he clearly awakened considerable hope and expectation. There was something different about him. After his first exorcism, in Mark's gospel, when the narrative has barely begun, we read that the people 'were amazed, and they kept on asking one another, "What is this? A new teaching – and with authority! He commands even the unclean spirits, and they obey him"' (Mark 1.27). And yet this adulation soon begins to turn sour, when the declaration of forgiveness he makes to a paralysed man draws forth an accusation of blasphemy from the scribes, on the grounds that God alone can forgive sin. The people, nevertheless, 'were all amazed and glorified God, saying, "We have never seen anything like this"' (Mark 2.1–12).

Much the same sort of thing occurs in Luke's gospel. The very first thing Jesus does as part of his public ministry is to go to the synagogue, where he reads from the prophecy of Isaiah. Having done so, he preaches his first sermon, claiming that the words of the prophet had been fulfilled in the hearing of the people there and then (Luke 4.16–30). Again, some were amazed at his words, but within just a few verses, others were taking him to throw him over a cliff in order to kill him. Why? How could the mood have turned so quickly?

Partly because he drew direct attention to the fact that in the history of the Jewish people, it appeared that it was often non-Jews – Gentiles – who were the recipients of God's favour rather than the Jews themselves. As examples, Jesus cites a widow of Zarephath in Sidon during the time of the prophet Elijah, and Naaman the Syrian, who was cured of leprosy at the time of the prophet Elisha. At least as significant as this, though, is that in the passage read from Isaiah (61.1–2a), he stops short of a crucial part of the second verse. Having identified himself by implication as the one who has been anointed by the Spirit, he reads that, in fulfilment of the prophecy, his vocation is to bring good news to the poor, release to the captives and recovery of sight to the blind. He concludes by reading that he is to 'proclaim the year of the Lord's favour' but omits what follows: 'and the day of vengeance of our God' (Isaiah 61.2). This would seem to account for the way in which the assembled company turns hostile. The Jewish people wanted vengeance for all that they had suffered over the centuries, and especially for what they were suffering now at the hands of the Romans, and yet here was Jesus implying that God was not concerned about vengeance. If that were so, the people would have to reconsider how they saw and experienced God, as well as those whom they excluded.

From the outset, then, Jesus seems deliberately to turn his back on popular expectations and resists falling prey to what was projected on to him. Why? For the reason that Jesus himself saw and experienced things differently. It was his mission to encourage and enable others to know God in the way that he did, and to see others not as threats but as fellow human beings. This vision was far too radical, though, especially for the establishment, and it was this that set in motion a train of events which would end with his death by crucifixion.

What was most uncomfortable about Jesus was that he was truly and authentically himself. His integrity shone, and continues to shine, through his words and actions, and supremely in his willingness to give everything – including his life – rather than compromise his own truth, for it was precisely in being utterly true to himself that he enabled the very ground of his being, the unfathomable abyss of the one he called 'Father', to be laid bare. It was because he was so 'grounded' that he was at one at the same time totally authentic. For those who made accommodations and compromises in order to save what they thought was their own skin, such integrity was profoundly threatening, challenging and uncomfortable, and it still is. It holds up a mirror before us and invites us to look at ourselves, to see who we really are, to discover – like Huiming – whether we are more prepared to be seduced by the outer trappings of power, status and reputation than to live our own truth, which, because it is our own truth is at one and the same time also universal. In other words, integrity forces us to see that we are in fact deluded, that we live in a fantasy world of our own making for much of the time and spend an inordinate amount of time and effort – and sometimes money, too – on maintaining such a world.

The ubiquity of delusion

Christian tradition has been struck from the very beginning that Jesus was someone entirely without delusion, or, to put it in Christian language, without sin. There was no inner division in him, no separation between his ground and the way that ground was manifested in him. And precisely because he was so truly himself, he acted not out of vengeance, not out of the three so-called poisons of greed, hatred and ignorance or delusion, but out of the love, compassion and wisdom which characterise our true nature – what Suzuki (1999) calls 'original mind' or 'big mind'. What Jesus does is to show us that we are deeply conflicted, and that the only way that this conflict can be overcome is by dying the Great Death. In his love and compassion, he identifies with all of us in our delusion, he mysteriously transforms it by being wholly identified with it, and reveals that Great Death is the way to Great Life.

There are two ways in particular in which we are deluded. The first is in failing to acknowledge that life is characterised by impermanence, and the second is that we have a separate self to maintain and protect. We create the illusion of a permanent, separate, independent, substantial self, and it was the way in which Jesus unmasked this delusion, showing just how much we invest in it, that stirred up the opposition against him. The paradox, of course, is that it is the very desire to annihilate Jesus that itself distances us from our true nature of love and compassion and reinforces our delusion. The love and compassion embodied in Jesus are the only things which can overcome delusion, because they enable the deluded self to awaken to its true nature, which is love and compassion. When our delusions are unmasked, we have a choice either to let them go or to project them onto whoever shows them for what they are. Jesus' death was brought about by the most intense collective and concerted action on the part of the religious and political establishment to preserve itself and its own delusions at all costs. They rejected the invitation to undergo the Great Death, and, in the process, rejected Great Life. And yet, because we are not separate from anyone or anything, when Jesus died, he died the Great Death for all, and when he rose from the dead, he rose to the Great Life for all, in much the same way that when Shakyamuni Buddha attained enlightenment, he did so not as a separate, individual self: he, the great earth, and all beings simultaneously achieved the Way.[5]

It can scarcely be said that Jesus was timid about the nature of impermanence. As he is presented in the gospels, he began to make it clear quite early on that he was destined to suffer and die. However, this met with huge resistance on the part of his disciples. Having predicted his passion and death for the first time, Peter took him aside and rebuked him, declaring that such a thing could never happen to Jesus. In response, Jesus' words are uncompromising: 'Get behind me Satan! For you are setting your mind not on divine things but on human things' (Mark 8.33). In order to reinforce the point, which the disciples still failed to grasp, the prediction is made again on two further occasions (Mark 9.30–32; 10.32–34).

Similarly, shortly before his passion, Jesus drew attention to the impermanence of the temple. In so doing, he will have awakened all the hurts, wounds and anxieties of centuries of deeply painful history. The temple was the primary symbol of God's presence and the focus of the people's identity. 'Do you see these great buildings? Not one stone will be left here upon another; all will be thrown down' (Mark 13.2), Jesus warned. It is not surprising that such plain speaking should have been met with resistance. It was the unpalatable doubt about the permanence of the temple – and, by implication, the very basis of what the people held most dear and on which they established their lives – which Jesus evoked, and that was subsequently turned against him in the form of a false accusation, as he stood before the high priest and others at his trial:

---

5   See Chapter 1.

Now the chief priests and the whole council were looking for testimony against Jesus to put him to death; but they found none. For many gave false testimony against him, and their testimony did not agree. Some stood up and gave false testimony against him, saying, 'We heard him say, "I will destroy this temple that is made with hands, and in three days I will build another not made with hands".' But even on this point their testimony did not agree. (Mark 14.55–59)

It is not surprising, perhaps, that because of the loss that the people had had to endure over the centuries, they hankered after a secure state, in which their collective identity would be permanently established, a state in which they would be vindicated and enabled to assert themselves over and against their enemies. Jesus challenged not only the delusion of permanence but also the delusion of separation and division in terms of friends and enemies. His celebrated parable, known as The Good Samaritan (Luke 10.25–37), does just this by exposing the way that prejudice against the Samaritans enabled the Jews to spin all sorts of narratives in an attempt to assert their own superiority over and against them, but to their own cost. As Jesus demonstrated, it was a foreigner, who, in coming to the assistance of a Jew in need, actually showed the compassion required by the Law: to love God and one's neighbour *as oneself* (Luke 10.27; Matthew 22.37–40; Mark 12.29–31). Compassion knows no bounds, and desires to meet human need in whatever shape or form it presents itself. Apart from depicting compassion in action, the primary purpose of the parable was surely that Jesus' audience should be prompted to look at themselves again and become aware of their delusions. We all tell stories about ourselves and others with the intention – even if only unconscious – of giving substance to the idea of a separate self, whether individual or collective. Such selves come to be exposed as fictions and delusions, as those in Jesus' audience, who were prepared to take to heart the full import of the parable, would have discovered. Such delusions only disappear insofar as we are prepared to undergo the Great Death.

When the fiction of a permanent, unchanging, separate self feels itself to be threatened to the point of extinction, it mobilises everything in its power to defend itself. This is precisely what happened in relation to Jesus. The religious authorities had come to an arrangement over time that they would conform to Roman rule, provided that there were certain dispensations in relation to their religious practices. Although they had received such concessions, the cost was the people's integrity. Such was Jesus' integrity that he showed up the lack of it on the part of the people as a whole, making it painfully clear that the *status quo* would have to be relinquished if life was to be lived authentically. What is evident in the Passion narratives in the gospels is that there are almost no lengths to which this threatened fictional self will not go to preserve itself. The Jewish establishment resorted to lies, deceit, falsehood, abuse, hatred, violence, aggression and sheer venom, in an attempt to maintain itself in collusion with the Roman authorities. In so doing, it also enlisted the help of the general populace by pandering to the basest instincts of the deluded self, stirring up the cries of 'Crucify!', uttered, perhaps, with little or no understanding on the part of those who shouted as to what was really going on at all.

Jesus becomes one with delusion

The most significant feature of it all, though, was how Jesus reacted to it. Rather than resist it or fight it, he embraced it and accepted it. He became completely one with it, and this is what is salvific. Jesus was faced with unimaginable physical, mental, psychological and spiritual pain. To say that he did not resist it is not to say that the pain went over his head, as it were, or that it did not really exist. Jesus received the full onslaught of the terrifying effects of delusion in all its aspects. What is meant by the assertion that Jesus did not resist it is that he entered into it fully. No doubt he screamed with pain, of course, but feeling the pain is part of not resisting it. In other words, he did not experience his pain as something separate from what his life was at that moment. Jesus himself will have had all sorts of expectations that his life would proceed in this way rather than that. Whatever stories he might have told himself, whatever ideas he might have entertained, in the end, reality for all of us is always different. It would appear that he even expected that he might have been saved and delivered from the experience by God, but even that was discovered to have been a projection that had to go, too: 'My God, my God, why have you forsaken me?' (Matthew 27.46; Mark 15.34). Granted, these words are part of Psalm 22, so we might assume that Jesus was reciting something that he already knew. The point remains, however, that it was with these words that he identified himself. His experience was one of God-forsakenness. He was left supremely alone, with nothing beyond himself to help.

This, however, is the startling significance. In letting go of his idea of God, Jesus died the Great Death, and at that very moment, in all his apparent God-forsakenness, was the very presence and embodiment of God. The God by whom Jesus is forsaken, the God who is conceived of as being external to ourselves, is revealed not to be God after all, but merely the idea or concept of a God as separate from us. On the cross there is no separation, no division, because, as the very presence and embodiment of God, Jesus accepts and embraces the totality of the situation. In so doing he is truly himself, the true self of all. He is the 'Lamb of God' (John 1.36), who takes away the sin of the world, because he is totally at one with it in its pain, suffering and delusion. He is compassion in the true sense of the word: the one who suffers with the whole of creation, and in so doing redeems it.

Connecting the Passion with the practice of *zazen*

Earlier on in this chapter I suggested that there was a difference between Jesus and Shakyamuni Buddha in the manner of their deaths. Shakyamuni Buddha died peacefully in his old age, while Jesus, as we have just been reminding ourselves, had to endure a very public, humiliating and painful death. At one level, these two deaths seem to have little or nothing in common with each other. The practice of *zazen*, however, can enable us to see that they do, for as we sit *zazen* on the mat, we enter into the experience which holds them together as one.

The expression, 'dying on the mat', is sometimes used in Zen. This refers to what is encountered when we take seriously the commitment to remain seated on the mat for the allotted period of time, come what may, however painful or uncomfortable the experience may be. Sometimes the desire to get off the mat and go and do anything other than just sit there can be overwhelming. During prolonged periods of sitting over several days, such as during a *sesshin* (an intensive retreat) for example, the physical pain experienced in one's knees and legs or elsewhere in the body, as a result of putting them under the kind of pressure to which they are not habitually accustomed, can be considerable. The decision to remain on the mat is borne not of a misplaced sense of masochism, but of a resolution to take responsibility for all that occurs on the mat and, therefore, for all that presents itself at every moment as one's life, which, on the mat, might well include a degree of physical pain. As it happens, what we learn is that it is the *idea* of the pain as experienced in our imagination, which is invariably far worse than the *actual* pain itself. We notice that we begin to tell ourselves stories about the pain, which has the paradoxical effect of intensifying the pain, and we discover that the pain is lessened when we give up fighting it and accept it instead. We let go of ourselves *into* the pain rather than away from it, and we become one with it.

Far more irksome than the physical pain, though, can be what we experience of who we really are at that moment. The kind of delusions that led to the demand for Jesus' death are ours, just as much as they were of the people involved at the time. When we are identified with the construct of a separate, unchanging, independent, substantial self, any threat to that identity is experienced as a threat to all that we are. And, of course, from that perspective, it is. We have to die. From the perspective of who we truly are, though, it is not. It is actually an invitation to awaken to our true self, which is characterised supremely by love, compassion and wisdom, the self which embraces everyone and everything.

The commitment to staying on the mat is the result of a prior decision made with the awareness, however slight, that we are more than we think we are or know ourselves to be in a limited sense. As we sit on the mat, we allow our delusions to make themselves felt, we let them come and go, we stay with them and let them be, in the faith and trust that, as Shakyamuni Buddha discovered, our own self-nature will manifest itself of its own accord, bringing freedom, joy and peace with it.

As we sit on the mat, we realise that Shakyamuni Buddha and Jesus both sit with us, so to speak. Metaphorically speaking, the cross is Jesus' mat, and the mat on which Shakyamuni Buddha sat under the Bodhi tree is the cross, just as the mat on which we sit is also our cross. As Shakyamuni Buddha sat under the Bodhi tree, he allowed his egotism to subside and his true self to emerge from deep within. As Jesus hung on the cross, he showed what that true self is in the most ghastly of circumstances. Jesus' dying and death show that love and compassion are what is there when there is no egotism, or, to express this in a characteristically Buddhist way, when there is no-self. Indeed, unless there is no-self, there can be no real love or compassion. This no-self, though, is not nothing. It is an emptiness, which is also a fullness. From this emptiness pours forth life endlessly and abundantly, just as three days after Jesus' death, life exploded from the emptiness of the tomb. It is into this dynamic that we enter every time we sit on the mat. We die in order to live.

Summary: and a final question

This chapter began with the story of Kisa Gotami, the young mother grieving for the death of her son, who learned for herself, at the compassionate and skilful hands of Shakyamuni Buddha, that there is no way that any of us can escape death. With reference to our own experience, to Jesus' story, and to various Zen *kōans*, it was suggested that life and death are mysteriously and ambiguously intertwined, such that it is not always clear which is which. In many ways, life can be seen as dying the Great Death, in the sense of continuously dying to the deluded fiction that we are an unchanging, permanent, independent, substantial self. When this 'self' dies, though, there is an awakening to everything as the self of all. In Zen terms, Jesus was never anything other than this self, original mind, big mind, something he revealed supremely on the cross by accepting and embracing delusion and suffering with love and compassion. In Christian terminology, the God to whom Jesus cried as the one who had forsaken him was shown to be nowhere other than where Jesus was: on the cross itself, in the person of Jesus himself and, therefore, completely at one with us. We realise this for ourselves through the practice of *zazen*, which entails the process of 'dying on the mat', of letting go of delusion, particularly in the form of the belief that we are a separate, independent, substantial, permanent self. From the emptiness that we experience as we die on the mat, life pours forth, an experience of resurrection coming to us from beyond, from the unfathomable abyss of the Father's love, something that cannot be manipulated or controlled, but only received.

It remains only to ask one final question. As we ponder the events of Jesus' Passion, and consider the various protagonists – the religious and political authorities, the crowd and Jesus himself – which of them were dead and which were alive? And what about us? Are we ourselves dead or alive?

PART 3

Living Your Own Life

Chapter 5

At Home with Oneself

Peter and John compared

The final chapter of the Gospel of John is focused, to a considerable extent, on the figure of Peter. At the beginning of the chapter, the disciples are gathered on a beach, when, from nowhere, the Risen Christ appears before them. While they have breakfast together, Jesus asks Peter three times whether he loves him or not. Peter makes three affirmations, after which Peter is told first, 'Feed my lambs', then, 'Tend my sheep', and finally, 'Feed my sheep' (John 21.15–17). Many have seen in this exchange the tender compassion of Christ in giving Peter the opportunity to make up for the three times, when, after Jesus had been arrested, he had denied that he was one of Jesus' followers (John 18.17, 25 and 27). If this is indeed how the episode is to be read, it suggests the most wonderful affirmation of Peter by Christ, who accepts Peter's frailty for what it is, but also sees that Peter is far more than this.

It might have been expected that after this intimate conversation between Jesus and Peter, in which Peter could not have been reassured any more than he was of Jesus' confidence in him, that Peter would have been completely self-assured. In what are almost the closing verses of the chapter, it appears, however, that this was far from the case:

> Peter turned and saw the disciple whom Jesus loved following them; he was the one who had reclined next to Jesus at the supper and had said, 'Lord, who is it that is going to betray you?' When Peter saw him, he said to Jesus, 'Lord, what about him?' Jesus said to him, 'If it is my will that he remain until I come, what is that to you? Follow me!' So the rumour spread in the community that this disciple would not die. Yet Jesus did not say to him that he would not die, but, 'If it is my will that he remain until I come, what is that to you?' (John 21.20–23)

It may well be that this passage reflects some very particular theological concerns of the Johannine community. Straight after Peter has been affirmed by Jesus in the verses immediately preceding this incident, Jesus has told Peter that when he grows old, he will stretch out his hands, and that someone else will put a belt around him and take him where he does not wish to go. Before telling Peter, 'Follow me', a comment has been inserted by the redactor, saying that Jesus had said this to 'indicate the kind of death by which he would glorify God' (John 21.18–19).

What is being presented to us in all this is a comparison between Peter and the one who reclined next to Jesus at the Last Supper, generally referred to as the beloved disciple, or John, with whom the Johannine community (the community out of which the text of the Gospel of John emerged) might well have had a historical link: 'Lord, what about him?' The theological concern would be this. Peter was something of an activist, who was eventually martyred by being crucified himself. John, by contrast, as the inspiration for the Johannine community, was more of a contemplative, so the question that occupied the community was whether there was an ideal, best or most authentic way of being a follower of Christ. Was it more true to Christ to follow him to martyrdom, like Peter, or to live out one's discipleship into old age, based on a way of life given primarily to contemplative prayer and study? The words that Jesus speaks, 'If it is my will that he remain until I come, what is that to you?', implicitly confirm that, although the way the community is following Christ is different from that of Peter, it is, nevertheless, perfectly authentic.

Even if we were to take the exchange at face value, the essential point would still hold. Peter appears to be looking over his shoulder at John, and this causes him to wobble: 'Lord, what about him?' His self-confidence is fragile and he needs reassurance. Jesus effectively tells him to stop comparing himself with others, to stop worrying about them, and live his own life.

Comparing ourselves with others

We do spend a great deal of time comparing ourselves with others, assessing how we measure up against them. This is just as true of organisations and institutions as it is of individuals. At one level, this can be helpful, not least because we can learn from others. In the deepest sense, however, it can be pernicious and debilitating, because it reinforces the idea that we cannot truly be ourselves and live our own lives. Wanting to do this might sound egocentric and selfish, but it is not, far from it. In Zen terms, it is living in accordance with our self-nature, which is, in itself, 'in tune with the fundamental structure of the universe' (Armstrong 2000, p.84), or the way things 'really are' (Armstrong 2000, p.75).[1] In Christian terms, it is being who we are in Christ, the one in whom all things come to be and without whom not one thing is made, the one who is the life which is the light of all people (John 1.3–4).

Failing to see this can result in pursuing one of two alternatives. The first is, indeed, an utterly egocentric approach to life, which springs from the desire to affirm our uniqueness and individuality by asserting ourselves over and against others, setting ourselves up in opposition to others. In truth, this actually flies in the face of common sense, which suggests that even at the most basic level of daily living, for example, we are all completely dependent on one another in all sorts of ways, whether that be for being nurtured as a baby at one end of the spectrum, to being cared for in sickness and old age at the other. The real price of egocentricity, however, is that we become separated from our self-nature, which is characterised through and through by profound interconnectedness and interrelationship.

The second possibility is that of simply copying and imitating others. In one sense, there is an important place for this. Children, for example, learn by copying. So, too, when someone is attempting to acquire a skill or a facility of some kind, copying those who have already advanced

---

1   See Chapter 1.

along a particular path is often precisely what is necessary. Creative artists, for example, learn precisely by engaging in exercises of pastiche, in order to discover from the inside, as it were, how a particular painter, writer or composer practised and mastered their art. What marks out all the great creative artists, though, is that in the process they discovered their own unique voice. As history shows, the expression of such a new voice has often been met initially with opprobrium and scorn, only to find itself lauded many years later. There can be huge pressure in society in general to conform and not step out of line, not least because people who are 'different' are so often perceived to be a threat. The price of this, however, is that we miss out on living our own lives in the way that only we can. The danger is that we can end up being little more than automata, half dead or lifeless.

Nor should it be thought that the so-called spiritual life is any different, as if slavishly imitating Jesus or Shakyamuni Buddha in every detail of their lives is the answer. That we can learn a great deal from them goes without question, and their example unquestionably sets us off in the right direction. Imitation, however, suggests something external to us that has to be imported, as it were, or added on, something that is not fundamentally us. Where Jesus and Shakyamuni Buddha are concerned, the relationship is far more intimate than imitation, it is internalised. However much we might learn at one level by imitation, the time comes when we know that we have to be not just a copy of someone else, but who we really are. Thus, although the apostle Paul invites the members of the Church in Corinth to be imitators of him as he is of Christ (1 Corinthians 11.1), his relationship to Christ is not that of someone outside himself. Rather, Christ is his life: 'I have been crucified with Christ; and it is no longer I who live, but it is Christ who lives in me' (Galatians 2.19b–20). Paul knew from bitter experience that truly being himself came not from a strict obedience to an externally prescribed law, but from being 'in Christ', and from being enlivened from within by the 'law of the Spirit of life in Christ Jesus', which 'has set you free from the law of sin and death' (Romans 8.1–2).

The importance of being ourselves rather than a pale imitation of someone else, however wonderful they might have been, is beautifully caught in a story told of the Polish Hasidic Master, Rabbi Meshulam Zusha (1718–1800). As he lay on his deathbed, surrounded by his disciples, he was crying inconsolably. When he was asked what possible reason he could have had for crying, because he had, after all, lived a wonderful life, becoming as wise as Moses and as kind as Abraham, he responded that when he passed from this world and stood before the heavenly tribunal, he would not be asked why he was not as wise as Moses or as kind as Abraham. Instead he would be asked: 'Zusha, why weren't you Zusha? Why didn't you follow the path that could have been yours?'[2]

Christianity and Zen each provide paths which enable us to be truly who we are. As we have seen, though, following these paths is not without challenges. It might be thought that having undergone the Great Death and having clarified the 'great matter of life and death', whether on the mat or on the cross, everything would thereafter

---

2   Rabbi Mushulam Zusha's reflections and commentaries were compiled by his students after his death in the *Menorat Zahav*. This story can be found online at http://rabbishimon.com/tzadikim/showz. php?p=zusha.htm.

be straightforward. Everything does look different, of course, but this does not necessarily mean that there is an immediate and enduring transformation, or that life is blissfully without its difficulties. This applies in the contexts of both Zen and Christianity alike. In both traditions, there is a recognition that awakening and change can be sudden or gradual. Those who come to faith in Christ as a result of a sudden conversion know all too well that the vestiges of the 'old self' still linger, sometimes to a significant and troubling extent. Similarly, those who experience *kensho* – a sudden awakening to their enlightenment – in Zen do not find that their way of life is changed immediately in all respects. Delusions remain, even if they are seen in a different light. So, too, in both traditions it is recognised that for some, perhaps the vast majority, there is nothing sudden about anything. There is just steady practice, in which, without thinking about it too much, one gradually embodies Christ or realises the Dharma.

Whether awakening is sudden or gradual in either tradition, its effect is that we are freed to be at home with ourselves, set at liberty to live our own lives. Like the Prodigal Son, we are to come to ourselves in the fullness of all that that entails.[3] From this point on in this chapter, I should like to consider how we do indeed come to ourselves ever more fully by looking at one more *kōan*, by examining in a little more detail what is involved in the practice of *zazen*, and by relating this to the practice of prayer in the Christian tradition. In the *kōan*, we meet an old friend, the great Zen Master Jōshū, whom we have already encountered previously.[4]

---

3   See Chapter 1.

4   See Chapter 4.

Jōshū Sees Through the Old Woman

The case

A monk asked an old woman, 'Which way should I take to Mount Gotai?' The old woman said, 'Go straight on'. When the monk had taken a few steps, she remarked, 'He may look like a fine monk, but he, too, goes off like that!'

Later a monk told Jōshū about it. Jōshū said, 'Wait a bit. I will go and see through that old woman for you.' The next day, off he went, and asked her the same question. The old woman, too, gave him the same reply. When he returned, Jōshū announced to the monks, 'I have seen through the old woman of Mount Gotai for you.'

Mumon's commentary

The old woman knew how to work out a strategy and win the victory while sitting in her tent. Yes she is not aware of the bandit stealing into her tent. Old Jōshū is skilful enough to creep into the enemy's camp and menace their fortress. Yet he does not look like a grown-up. Upon close examination, they are both at fault. Now tell me, how did Jōshū see through the old woman?

The verse

The question is the same each time,
The answer, too, is the same.
In the rice there is sand,
In the mud there are thorns.

(Shibayama 2000, pp.223–224;
Yamada 2004, p.153)

The *kōan* at surface level

This *kōan* may initially seem rather perplexing, so we have to recognise that, like all *kōans*, it is operating on several levels at once. On the surface, it concerns a monk who is making a pilgrimage to Mount Gotai, also known as Mount Wutai or simply Mount Tai, and an old woman, who probably owns a tea shop on the pilgrimage route, and whom he passes on his way. The significance of Mount Gotai in north-eastern China is that it is said to be the dwelling place of the great bodhisattva of wisdom, Manjuśrī. In iconography, Manjuśrī is depicted as wielding a sword to cut off ignorance and delusion in one hand, and a text relating to *prajñāpāramitā*, the supreme wisdom, in the other hand. On the face of it, therefore, the monk seems to be no different from the millions of people across the ages, who have made, and who continue to make, pilgrimages to holy sites, with the intention of deepening their faith, fulfilling an obligation, or renewing their commitment in some way.

Making a pilgrimage to Mecca, for example, is one of the Five Pillars of Islam, and Muslims endeavour to make such a pilgrimage at least once in their lifetime, if circumstances allow. Similarly, Christians make pilgrimages to the Holy Land to visit sites associated with the life of Christ, or walk the *Camino* to Santiago de Compostela in Spain, or journey to Lourdes in France in search of healing. Sikhs go on pilgrimage to the Golden Temple at Amritsar, and Hindus, too, make pilgrimages to Varanasi to bathe in the sacred waters of the River Ganges, as well as to many other places. In the present day, pilgrimage seems to be undergoing something of a revival in Christian circles, so the whole notion of pilgrimage has a longstanding pedigree. In this sense, the monk represents something universal in human experience – a search for wisdom, truth, enlightenment and faith.

There is something rather odd about the question the monk puts to the old woman, though. Presumably he was walking a well-trodden route. Many other people would have been making the same pilgrimage as he was. So why does he stop to ask the way? If the woman owned a teashop, then she might have represented the welcome opportunity to have some refreshment and a short respite. Perhaps he asked the question just to reassure himself, but it would seem that there was some doubt in his mind, a lack of conviction or security, a hesitation of some kind, and he needed someone else to confirm that he was going in the right direction. It has been suggested, for example, that the old woman's teashop stood at a fork in the road (Yamada 2004, p.154) or at a crossroad (Brown Hedgpeth 2013, p.18). In which case, what help would 'Go straight on' have been?

The *kōan* at a deeper level

It is at this point that another level opens up to us, for we might see the monk's pilgrimage as symbolic of a deeper quest, the pursuit of his true self, a search for who he really was. The question arises, therefore, as to whether he would have been any nearer finding his true self as a result of making this pilgrimage or not. What would his true self look like? How would he know when he had found it? Many pilgrims were said to have returned with stories of having received visions of one kind or another on Mount Gotai. Was the monk looking and hoping for some special kind of experience that would confirm that he was on the right lines or that would mark him out as special in some sort of way? Did he feel that something was missing in his life that the pilgrimage would provide?

At a superficial level, the woman gives him a straightforward answer to his question: 'Just go straight on!' She might just as well have said, 'Just follow the crowd. Can't you see, they're all going in the same direction?' Her response, however, suggests something rather more subtle. After the monk has taken just a few steps, it is as if she notices that he is actually going in the *wrong* direction: 'He may look like a fine monk, but he, too, goes off like that!' There is something of a barb in her remark. Outwardly, the monk seems to be doing everything just right in his life – he is, after all, following the monastic path in a dedicated way – but she can see that he is misguided in some way. If this is the case, what does 'Go straight on' mean? Where and how is he is going to find who he really is, his true self? It is as if she is saying that on this level, he is not going to find what he is looking for by searching for it outside himself, or somewhere other than where he is at that very moment. So, we might ask: at that very instant, who was he and where was he in his life? What was presenting itself to him at that precise moment as his life, and what was he failing to see? And that same question can just as well be asked of us right now. In which case, what does 'Go straight on' mean in your life and mine, here and now?

A hint is given to us in what follows in the case. The story proceeds with another monk telling the great Master Jōshū about the other monk's encounter with the old woman. There are a number of implications here. There is nothing about whether the monk continued on his way to Mount Gotai. Did he turn back and discontinue the journey or did he go on and find what he was looking for? It would seem, however, that his ego was bruised somewhat by the encounter, for it would appear that, when he returned, he told the other monks about what had happened: 'Do you know what, I came across this old woman at a teashop on the pilgrimage route, and all I did was politely ask her the way and she just put me down. Who does that old woman think she is, and what does she know about anything anyway?'

This is surely a common scenario for all of us. Someone else says or does something that calls us into question in some way, and rather than being open to the possibility of the truth that is being presented, we get all uppity, brittle and defensive, and focus on the inadequacies and shortcomings of the other person. We instinctively feel superior and look to others to reassure us. The very fact that we do so suggests a degree of doubt in our own minds as to whether we really are right. It was something of this syndrome that was touched on earlier in relation to Peter and John, where, despite the fact that Peter had been the recipient of the unconditional love of the Risen Christ, he still compared himself with John, and asked where he stood in relation to him. In any case, what happened to the monk on his way to Mount Gotai seems to have affronted all of his fellow monks, too, and this in turn prompted one of them, in solidarity with the monk's hurt pride, to mention the incident to Jōshū, as if to suggest that the woman needed to be put in her place. If this were so, what would the issue have been?

An enlightened woman?

There was always the suspicion that some women were really Zen masters in disguise. It is salutary to be reminded that, although it was affirmed from the beginning that all beings are endowed with Buddha nature, women were somehow treated, nevertheless, as being inferior, something that is only really coming to be redressed in our own time in Zen, as well as in other religious traditions, to say nothing of society in general.[5] The question for the monks, then, would have been this: despite the seeming sharpness of her tongue, was this otherwise rather unprepossessing old woman truly enlightened or not? In order to find out, they had to ask Jōshū.

So a second question arises: how would they have been able to tell whether she or anyone else was enlightened? And why were they unable to see for themselves? The answer can only be, as was the case with Huiming, that nothing more is needed than to taste whether the water is cold or warm.[6] Do we need someone else to tell us? Can we not taste it for ourselves? What does the litchi taste like when it is in our mouth?[7] What else could possibly add to the taste itself? The monks could not smell what was right under their noses, they were unable to see what was right there before them. They were blinded by the delusion of their own prejudice. Not only could they not see the woman for who she truly was, neither had they settled, as it were, into themselves. They were not yet at home with

---

5   Illuminating examples of attempts to raise the profile of women in this regard are Caplow and Moon (2013) and Toomey (2015).

6   See Chapter 4.

7   See Chapter 4.

who they really were. Had they been, there would have been no need for them to initiate the elaborate charade which followed.

Jōshū plays along with them and goes to check out the old woman. In truth, he must have known already. He would have been able to tell, from the way the whole incident came to his attention, that it was the prickliness and insecurity of his monks that was really at play here. The fragility of their egos and their need for affirmation from outside themselves would not have been hidden from him; he was able to see through it all. Suppose, though, that he had simply told them that she really was a Zen master in disguise, in what way could that possibly have helped? Would they thereby have been able to see? If they were unable to see it already, no amount of telling would have been able to help. Unless they could taste and smell it for themselves, they would have been none the wiser. For this reason, Jōshū strings them along. As will be clear, he refrained from telling them anything at all, except that he had 'seen through the old woman of Mount Gotai' for them. What, then, had he seen through? It was just this that he left the monks to work out for themselves.

It will be noticed that he asked the same question of the woman as did the monk, and that he received exactly the same reply. Yet, the question and the answer in relation to Jōshū amounted to something different, in contrast to that given to the monk. As the verse says, 'The question is the same each time, the answer, too, is the same. In the rice there is sand, in the mud there are thorns.' What is this getting at?

There is something of a clue in Mumon's commentary here. The old woman is likened to a general sitting in his tent, working out how to defeat the enemy far away on the battlefield, but who or what is the enemy and what is she doing other than sitting there and serving tea to passing pilgrims? The assertion that Jōshū 'does not look like a grown-up' suggests that he is behaving rather like a child, not ignorantly or childishly so much as with a considerable degree of playfulness. There is the innocence of a child playing a game for the sheer fun of it here. Perhaps we can imagine Jōshū and the old woman taking a look at each other and giving one another a knowing look, a wink of the eye, a grin, a cheeky smile, as if to acknowledge the tacit realisation that they are both up to no good, that they 'are both at fault'. Not only did Jōshū see through the old woman, she saw through him, too. So what did they do? What would it have been for them both to 'go straight on' in these circumstances? Perhaps the old woman said to him, 'You're a fine monk, but off you go just like the rest of them!' The tone of voice would have been a giveaway, though. She would have been able to indicate that she could see through him and see that he was not actually just like the rest of them. In response, perhaps Jōshū did a little jig or something rather random to show that he could see through her. What did they see, though?

Nothing more and nothing less than that they were perfectly at home with themselves and, therefore, with each other. All that was necessary for them was to respond naturally and spontaneously to what was presented to both of them at that moment. What would have been the most obvious and natural thing in the world to do? She, after all, ran a teashop. Surely they would simply have just had a cup of tea together.

So what was it that the monk on pilgrimage and his fellow monks were unable to see? Like us, it would seem, they assumed that enlightenment was something extraordinary, elaborate, complicated, difficult and special, which had to be achieved and found somewhere else. From one perspective, it does indeed seem to be all those things. The truth is, though, that from another perspective it is utterly ordinary and simple. It is just who we are and what life is right now. There is no need to seek it anywhere other than where we are just at this moment. Indeed, doing other than that is to encounter one obstacle after another. It is like cooking sand in the hope of getting rice. How daft could that be? If we do that, it will be like being pricked by thorns in the mud. There is no need to add anything to what is. Enlightenment is 'just this'. All we have to do is wake up to it.

Experience tells us that we so easily think that it cannot possibly be as simple as just being at home with ourselves. We all find this so difficult to believe, and we torment ourselves with assumptions and expectations that we have to be other than who we are, or add something to ourselves that we believe we lack in order to make up for purported deficiencies. From a Zen point of view, *the purpose of practice is precisely to discover that we do not have to practise to become enlightened; we are enlightened already.* All we have to do is realise it and live it. Does that mean that we have to abandon things like pilgrimages? No, not at all. We simply have to abandon the notion that making a pilgrimage will add to our already inherently enlightened state. If we go on a pilgrimage, we go on a pilgrimage for the sake of going on a pilgrimage and enjoying it for its own sake, and not to become enlightened. We realise our enlightenment right where we are at any given moment. There is no need to be or to go somewhere else to attain it.

This is exactly what *zazen* shows us. The practice of *zazen* is encouraged not because enlightenment is thereby achieved. It is simply the manifestation of enlightenment in the most natural way. What is discovered through the practice of *zazen* is lived out in every circumstance and situation of life. So let us look in a little more detail than we have done so far at what happens when we sit *zazen*.

The practice of *zazen*

Towards the beginning of this book, I recalled an occasion when I had visited the website of a Zen centre and viewed video footage of people sitting *zazen*. It occurred to me that for anyone unfamiliar with the practice of *zazen*, the whole scene might well have looked rather strange. It would probably have raised all sorts of questions about what was going on and what its purpose was.[8] I then invited you to get a taste for yourself of what was actually happening by introducing you to the practice of *zazen* through a simple exercise.[9] Reflecting on what that experience might have been like for you, I proposed that among the various things that it might have thrown up was a question: who am I? I suggested that the practice of *zazen* enables us to discover the answer to that question by 'doing nothing', and that the answer is experienced as a coming home to ourselves, the realisation of who we truly are.[10]

---

8   See Chapter 1.

9   See Chapter 1.

10   See Chapter 1.

In the interests of avoiding misunderstanding, this perhaps needs some further clarification. 'Doing nothing' could so easily look like an abdication of responsibility for one's life and all that it entails, a turning of one's back on the immense suffering and injustice that there is in the world, for example, rather than seeking to respond compassionately to it. And yet the practice of *zazen* itself is extraordinarily powerful in making it possible for us to awaken to who we actually are. So let us clarify what this 'doing nothing' is in the context of *zazen*. Before going any further, it might be helpful to be reminded of how *zazen* is practised. The instructions are essentially very simple: sit still, settle into your body, pay attention to the breath, and let go of thought by allowing what arises in the mind just to come and go. When you get hooked by a thought, notice it, let it go, and gently return to the breath.

Whether you practise *zazen* regularly or not, little more than a moment's reflection will make it abundantly clear that there is, in fact, a 'doing something' going on here. For a start, there is a clear intention not just to sit, but to sit attentively, and this in itself requires a degree of energy and concentration. Effort of a kind is needed in order to sit still and retain one's physical posture without moving in response to every itch, niggle or more serious discomfort. So, too, is it necessary to maintain a strength and continuity of awareness, if we are not to get hooked by thoughts and succumb to something that would be tantamount to daydreaming. That might very well be a pleasant, interesting or amusing distraction, but *zazen* it most certainly is not. Once the mechanics of *zazen* are in place, though, the essential practice is indeed 'doing nothing', and this 'doing nothing' enables us to be who we are, to realise our true self.

Dōgen on *zazen*

In his *Fukan Zazengi*, Zen Master Dōgen makes the bold claim that the simple practice of *zazen*, in all its physical and mental aspects, actually enables us to awaken to and manifest 'ultimate reality':

> When your body posture is correct, breathe in and out [once, deeply]. Sway left and right [several times] and then sit firmly and resolutely. Think about the unthinkable. How do you think about the unthinkable? Non-thinking. These are the essentials of *zazen*.
>
> That which we call *zazen* is not a way of developing concentration. It is simply the comfortable way. It is practice that measures your *satori* to the fullest, and is in fact *satori* itself.[11] It is the manifestation of the ultimate reality, and in it you will no longer be trapped as in a basket or a cage. If you understand my meaning [and do *zazen* correctly], you will be like a dragon who has reached the water, or like a tiger who trusts in the mountain where he dwells. Know that the true Dharma itself is present [in *zazen*], and that confusion and distraction are eradicated right from the beginning. (Cook 2002, pp.66–67)

Dōgen captures the sense of 'doing nothing' in his phrase, 'non-thinking'. At the same time, however, he

---

11   *Satori* is a Japanese word meaning 'awakening'. It is often translated as 'enlightenment'.

directs us to 'think about the unthinkable'. This is likely to be rather baffling. How can we think the unthinkable and simultaneously engage in non-thinking? It might be helpful, therefore, to probe what this entails and how 'non-thinking' awakens us to who we are.

Zazen: sky and clouds

When we practise *zazen*, we immediately become aware of what is going on in our minds. Sometimes what we are confronted with is little short of a teeming mass of thoughts. Any attempt to stop such thoughts is almost instantly acknowledged as being not just counter-productive but an impossibility; thoughts just come and go. *Zazen* involves not the suppression of thoughts, but rather letting go of them, and this is what Dōgen means by 'non-thinking'.

There is a distinction between a thought and the process of thinking. As we sit *zazen*, we notice that all sorts of thoughts arise in the mind. Most of them just come and then go. It is as if the mind is the sky and thoughts are the clouds passing across it. On occasions, the sky is clear and bright with few clouds to be seen. When it is like this, thoughts arise that are barely related to each other. We momentarily remember something, we register a sound, we notice our hunger, but they do not arise in a consequential way. They can seem almost to be rather random. As such, there is no process of thinking, which is to say, one thought leading inevitably to another in a rational way. Because of this, these thoughts do not disturb us, nor do we engage with them. They do not exert a great hold on our attention and it is fairly straightforward simply to let them go.

On other occasions, clouds seem to occupy the whole expanse of the mind. One cloud or thought leads almost seamlessly into the next and we can be scarcely aware of the fact. Thoughts simply follow and sometimes seem to chase after each other in a logical or related way. Before long, we realise that our *zazen* has simply been nothing other than thinking. There has been no letting go, no enabling of a space in which thoughts arise, just thoughts themselves.

Sometimes, though, it can feel even worse than that. Not only do clouds occupy the whole expanse of the sky, the sky can be stormy and angry and the clouds dark and billowy. When the mind is like this, it feels as if we are being besieged and overwhelmed. We can be aware of whole dramas and soap operas of our own creation taking place in the mind, imaginary monologues, dialogues and discussions, memories of past hurts or joys, the pains and wounds of relationships gone wrong, resentments and bitterness, and so much more. When *zazen* is like this, we become identified with any or all of these thoughts. There is no more to us than this. This is who we feel we are.

Paradoxically, for all that such things can be profoundly disturbing, causing us to long for the *zazen* to be different, *zazen* is not actually about getting rid of thoughts like these. In one sense, it is simply in the nature of the mind that such things should arise, just as it is natural that clouds should pass across the sky. The temptation to beat oneself up about the fact that one's mind is like this can be overwhelming, but what is really required is a compassionate self-acceptance. Little by little, *zazen* enables this to happen, as we resume the practice of letting go. Acceptance of oneself – and, indeed, of others – comes from the empty space which manifests itself in *zazen*.

Zazen: three scenarios in relation to thinking and non-thinking

Imagine, for a moment, someone who has never experienced themselves as other than their thoughts; they are wholly identified with them. Such a person is likely to be pushed and blown around from one thought to the next, acting and reacting on the basis of whatever arises. They are irritated by someone, so they punch them. They like the look of another, so they make a pass at them. Most of us are unlikely to live our lives in such an instinctive and unreflective way. Some do, however, almost wholly, and land themselves in considerable trouble as a result. All of us live that way to an extent. Something or someone can 'push our buttons', and in an instant we are totally identified with and consumed by whatever thought arises in response, lacking any control over our reactions, and finding ourselves having to pick up the pieces later. Being identified with our thoughts in this way can be truly disastrous, as, no doubt, we all know so well from our own experience and, perhaps, to our cost.

Imagine next, then, that someone who has never experienced themselves as other than their thoughts is introduced to *zazen*. The instruction is simple and always the same: focus on your breath, let your thoughts arise, let them come and go however disturbing or otherwise they may be, do not try to suppress them, but do not engage with them either. When you notice that you have been engaging with your thoughts, that you have been 'thinking', though, do not judge yourself harshly or even at all, but gently come back to the breath. It does not matter how many times you have to do this, just maintain the process.

What is happening here is the creation of a space that allows a detachment from thoughts. We tend to assume that we are our thoughts and identify ourselves with them. Disidentifying from them enables us to perceive that we are actually far more than our thoughts. Identifying ourselves with them limits us and prevents us from seeing that we are actually amazingly expansive. We are much more like the sky across which the clouds pass, than like the clouds themselves. When we see only the clouds – when we are identified wholly with our thoughts – we are unaware of the larger expanse of the sky in which the clouds float. From the perspective of the broad expanse of the sky, then, someone who is introduced to the practice of *zazen* will become gradually less governed by the incessant chatter of their mind and the habitual and instinctive responses that they make to people and circumstances, and what emerges is a wonderful sense of peace and calm.

Imagine, finally, that such a person continues to practise *zazen*. That person has experienced at first-hand on occasion that they are more than their thoughts, and yet thoughts continue to arise, sometimes furiously, as they did when the practice of *zazen* was taken up in the first place. What is the difference, then, between this experience and the experience of when they were wholly identified with their thoughts, for to all intents and purposes they sound and look just the same? The answer lies in the fact that the disidentification from one's thoughts, the distance that emerges between one's thoughts and oneself, makes all the difference in the world, for it results, so it seems, in a changed landscape. Thoughts can be seen and accepted for what they are, as no more and no less than the natural functioning of the mind. Clouds are, indeed, part of who we are, but they can come and go without causing too much disturbance. Whereas before there seemed to be nothing but thought, now there is space – an infinitely empty space, like an empty sky – which contains, holds and embraces our thoughts. It is this vast expanse of emptiness, and not our thoughts alone, which constitutes who we really are. Beyond the endless activity of the mind, there is a stillness. Beyond the incessant chatter and noise of the mind, there is silence. Beyond the superficial disturbances of the mind, there is a peace which passes all understanding.[12] Beyond and as the context of all this, there is what Christians refer to as 'God'.

On not identifying God with thoughts about God

Just as it is so easy for us to assume that we are our thoughts, so we can so easily misidentify God with our thought. To know God as God, though, we have to pass beyond thought, indeed, to do exactly what *zazen* invites. In his 29th German sermon, for example, the great medieval theologian, contemplative and mystic, Meister Eckhart (c.1260–c.1328), examines just this. God, he states, is ultimately nameless, for 'no one can either speak of him or know him'. Any statement affirming that God is good, wise or even that God exists is untrue because God is 'being beyond being: he is a nothingness beyond being'. He continues:

---

12   See Philippians 4.7.

Therefore St Augustine says: 'The finest thing that we can say of God is to be silent concerning him from the wisdom of inner riches.[13] Be silent, therefore, and do not chatter about God, for by chattering about him, you tell lies and commit a sin. If you wish to be perfect and without sin, then do not prattle about God. Also you should not wish to understand anything about God, for God is beyond all understanding. A master says: If I had a God I could understand, I would not regard him as God. If you understand anything about him, then he is not in it, and by understanding something of him, you fall into ignorance, and by falling into ignorance, you become like an animal, since the animal part in creatures is that which is unknowing. If you do not wish to become like an animal, therefore, do not pretend that you understand anything of the ineffable God.

'What then should I do?'

You should sink your 'being-you' into his 'being-him', and your 'you' and his 'him' should be a single 'me', so that with him you shall know in eternity his unbecome 'isness' and his unnameable 'nothingness'. (Davies 1994, pp.236–237)

Eckhart is clearly straining to say in words what simply cannot be said using words, for in the moment that words are spoken about God, the limitless reality of God is limited and the transcendent mystery of God is reduced to a thought. Just as the emptiness experienced

---

13 Davies notes that this should be attributed not to Augustine but to Pseudo-Denys, in his *Mystical Theology*, Chapter One, Paragraph One (Davies 1994, p.291).

in *zazen* is itself beyond thought and words, so is God. Indeed, the convergence between what is experienced in *zazen* and what Eckhart describes is either remarkable or unremarkable, depending on what is to be expected. In the Christian tradition, it is primarily in the practice of contemplative prayer that the parallel to *zazen* is found, so, in this, the final part of the chapter, let us very briefly turn to this.

Christian contemplative prayer

In recent years, contemplative prayer has enjoyed something of a revival, after it was significantly undervalued and obscured to a very considerable extent in the aftermath of the Reformation. Broadly speaking, it has flourished in the contemporary Church in two forms: Centring Prayer, as promoted by Fr Thomas Keating OCSO (Order of Cistercians of the Strict Observance), and Christian Meditation, as 'rediscovered' by Fr John Main OSB (Order of Saint Benedict). The latter is based on the simple practice of repeating an Aramaic phrase, 'Maranatha' – 'Come, Lord. Come, Lord Jesus' (Main 1980, p.53) – from the last book of the Bible (Revelation 22.20), with each breath, rather like a mantra in Hinduism. John Main actually discovered the practice of reciting a mantra from a Hindu Swami in Malaysia, 'which profoundly influenced the rest of his life' (McKenty 1986, pp.49–53). It was years later, after becoming a Benedictine monk, and having despaired of finding anything in the Christian tradition resembling what he had been taught in Malaysia, that he came across an almost identical practice in the lives of the fourth-century desert fathers and mothers, and particularly in the

Conferences of John Cassian, who advocated the simple practice of repeating a verse from a psalm: 'O Lord, come to my aid'.[14]

Thomas Keating – along with Fr Basil Pennington OCSO and Fr William Meninger OCSO – developed the practice of Centring Prayer during the 1960s, in response to the many people who visited their monastery in Snowmass, Colorado, in search of something in the Christian tradition akin to what they had come across on their travels in India and elsewhere. Thomas Keating advocates the practice of using a 'sacred word', which does not function in quite the same way as a mantra, in the sense that it is only reverted to when one discovers that one's mind has 'wandered', at which point the 'sacred word' is taken up again, until it 'drops out'. Indeed, using a word is not even necessary:

> A general loving look toward God may be better suited to the disposition of some persons. But the same procedures are followed as in the use of the sacred word. The word is sacred because it is the symbol of your intention to open yourself to the mystery of God's presence beyond thoughts, images and emotions. It is chosen not for its content but for its intent. It is merely a pointer that expresses the direction of your inward movement toward the presence of God. (Keating 1986, p.110)

---

14 The numbering of psalms varies. Roman Catholics have followed the Hebrew numbering since 1969, which means that the verse Cassian refers to is Psalm 69:2 (Cassian 1985, p.132). Anglicans and others adhere to the Greek practice of numbering psalms, so that the psalm in this case is 70:1. Anglicans, especially, will be familiar with this verse from the versicles and responses sung at Matins and Evensong according to the *Book of Common Prayer*: 'O God, make speed to save us; O Lord, make haste to help us'.

Anyone familiar with the anonymous fourteenth-century English treatise on contemplative prayer, *The Cloud of Unknowing* – to which further reference is made below – will notice that Centring Prayer is in many ways a contemporary re-visioning of the approach to prayer contained therein (Keating 1992, p.1).[15]

John Main was overjoyed to discover that the practice of contemplative prayer is deeply rooted in the Bible. As he suggests, Jesus himself may have been in the habit of using something like a mantra, which would account for the fact that he is described as praying before his arrest in the Garden of Gethsemane 'in the same words' (Main 1980, p.52; see Mark 14.39, Matthew 26.44). Furthermore, Main notes that whenever Jesus 'addresses the Father for the sake of the crowd, the word "Abba" is always on his lips, the same word which the apostle Paul describes the Spirit of Jesus eternally crying in our hearts' (Main 1980, p.52).[16]

Many, perhaps, will have been introduced to such prayer after being directed to take a well-known verse from Psalm 46 as the anchor to hold their attention on God: 'Be still, and know that I am God' (Psalm 46.10). At first glance, the word 'know' would seem to suggest that this is a direction to *think* about God. This would be completely foreign to Eckhart's instruction, though, and entirely out of keeping with the practice of *zazen*. 'Knowing' in the biblical sense, however, is far removed from 'thinking'. It entails intimacy, union and communion, it transcends

---

15   In addition to the two works already cited (Keating 1986 and 1992), a third (Keating 1987) forms a trilogy by relating contemplative practice to the liturgy.

16   For examples of how Main roots the practice of Christian Meditation in the Bible, see Main 1984 and 1985, especially the former.

thought and is often used of sexual intercourse, as in: 'Now the man knew his wife Eve, and she conceived and bore Cain' (Genesis 4.1). Knowledge and love, therefore, are closely bound up with each other.

Love, though, can only arise out of the poverty of emptiness, from the absence of egocentricity, selfishness and self-centredness, when the attention of one's whole being is entirely focused on the 'other'. Indeed, true love entails the loss of oneself in the other and a simultaneous finding of oneself in and as the other. Christians, therefore, regard the supreme manifestation and embodiment of love in the self-emptying on the cross of Jesus himself. Thus Paul writes to the Christians in Philippi, saying:

> Let the same mind be in you that was in Christ Jesus, who, though he was in the form of God, did not regard equality with God as something to be exploited, but emptied himself, taking the form of a slave, being born in human likeness. And being found in human form, he humbled himself and became obedient to the point of death – even death on a cross. (Philippians 2.5–8)

Paul continues to say that on account of this voluntary humiliation, God has given him the name that is above every name. 'Name' in the biblical sense, however, is far more than the word used to identify someone, just as knowing is far more than thinking. It is who they are, their very being. The name of Jesus, then, is not so much the word itself, as what Jesus shows he is, and this is none other than the love which emerges from emptiness.

Thus when Philip says to Jesus, 'Lord, show us the Father and we shall be satisfied', Jesus responds by saying:

Have I been with you all this time, Philip, and you still do not know me? Whoever has seen me has seen the Father. How can you say, 'Show us the Father?' Do you not believe that I am in the Father and the Father is in me? (John 14.8–10)

In a sense, Philip could have said to Jesus, 'Tell us God's real name, tell us who God really is', and Jesus could just as easily have replied, 'If you want to know God's name, look no further than me. I am God's name in my very being.' So what does Jesus reveal God's name to be? The self-emptying, self-giving love, which is the opposite of grasping, clinging, grabbing, controlling and fixing. It is in the image of this love that we are created. Contemplative prayer or meditation in the Christian tradition, therefore, is, like *zazen*, the practice of letting go of self, and awakening to and embodying love, compassion and wisdom as *who we are*.

Further clarification about what is meant by 'be still' in Psalm 46 comes from the Hebrew scholar, Robert Alter, who argues that a better translation of 'be still' is 'let go'. The context of the psalm is the battlefield and it is a warrior who is being encouraged to 'let go': '*Let go*. This verb – etymologically it means to relax one's grip on something – is somewhat surprising here. It might be an injunction to cease and desist from armed struggle, to unclench the warrior's fist' (Alter 2007, p.165). What this implies is that God's being, character and identity are known in the very process of letting go itself. It might almost be said that God is the letting go, and that we know God as the letting go, for God is always beyond whatever we try to cling and hold on to, including thought. God is known – and loved – therefore, in and as emptiness.

This is very much what is alluded to in the medieval treatise on contemplative prayer, *The Cloud of Unknowing*. The anonymous author says:

> But now you will ask me, 'How am I to think of God himself, and what is he?' and I cannot answer you except to say 'I do not know!' for with this question you have brought me into the same darkness, the same cloud of unknowing where I want you to be! For though we through the grace of God can know fully about all other matters, and think about them – yes, even the very works of God himself – yet of God himself can no man think. Therefore I will leave on one side everything I can think, and choose for my love that thing which I cannot think! Why? Because he may well be loved, but not thought. By love he can be thought and held, but by thinking never. Therefore, though it may be good sometimes to think particularly about God's kindness and worth, and though it may be enlightening too, and a part of contemplation, yet in the work now before us it must be put down and covered by a cloud of forgetting. And you are to step over it resolutely and eagerly, with a devout and kindling love, and try to penetrate that darkness above you. Strike that thick cloud of unknowing with the sharp dart of longing love, and on no account whatever think of giving up. (Wolters 1961, pp.59–60)

Not only does this resonate entirely with Eckhart's teaching about God, it is also – not surprisingly, of course – what seems to lie behind some of Jesus' teaching on prayer.

In the Sermon on the Mount, for example, he instructs his disciples that when they pray, they should not make a great show of things but that they should go into their room and pray to the Father 'who is in secret' (Matthew 6.6). In other words, God is hidden beyond what can be said or known. Similarly, Jesus invites his disciples to practise stillness of mind and heart by refraining from 'heaping up empty phrases as the Gentiles do; for they think that they will be heard because of their many words' (Matthew 6.7). Most importantly, Jesus suggests that none of this is necessary because God knows what we need before we ask him. In other words, everyone and everything is already suffused with God's presence; we just have to open ourselves to it. Such words as Jesus does give are those contained in the Lord's Prayer, the spirit of which, it might be said, consists in the giving up of one's small, egocentric concerns in order that God's will be done. The practice of *zazen*, too, entails just this: the letting go of all that we identify with and limit ourselves to, in order that the true self might be realised and manifested.

Zazen and Trinitarian experience

When John Main first articulated what Christian meditation was all about, he suggested that in learning to meditate we 'must pay attention firstly to ourselves', so that we might 'become fully aware of who we are', for 'we have a divine origin' (Main 1980, pp.3–4). Importantly, the purpose of meditation is 'not just to think about God, but to be with God, to experience God as the ground of our being' (Main 1980, p.5). Not surprisingly, Main's approach to Christian meditation is thoroughly grounded in Trinitarian theology and experience. The question arises, therefore: is it possible to relate to the experience of Zen from the perspective of Trinitarian experience? The answer to this question is, I suggest, affirmative, and in two ways. The first corresponds to what in the technical language of Trinitarian theology is called the economic Trinity, which is to say how God is revealed in the created order as Father, Son and Holy Spirit by virtue of what God does. The second relates to what is extrapolated from that about God's own inner being, what God is, which is referred to as the immanent Trinity. I want to suggest that the practice of *zazen* can be appreciated from a Christian perspective along these lines. In so doing, I am emphatically not wishing to 'colonise' Zen on behalf of Christianity. Zen has its own integrity and is to be practised for its own sake. When it is so practised, though, it can offer immeasurable riches to the Christian, which is what I am wanting to show throughout this book. Let us first consider the practice of Zen, then, in terms of the economic approach to the Trinity.

The basic practice of *zazen*, as we have seen, is simply following the breath, accepting what arises in the mind but gently letting it go and engaging with none of it. In the language of Christian spirituality, paying attention to the breath opens us to the presence of the Holy Spirit, the 'giver of life', as the Nicene Creed puts it, beyond all we can think or conceive. In terms of the Hebrew of the Old Testament and the Greek of the New Testament, *ruach* and *pneuma* can be translated as breath, wind or spirit alike. To attend to the breath, therefore, inevitably aligns us with and opens us to the very source of life, the Holy Spirit.

The experience of everyone who does this is, paradoxically, that the rational mind inevitably protests.

Simply being attentive to the breath strips us of all that we employ in support of our egocentric attitudes, impulses and identities. In this sense, it invites us to die to self, to be identified with Christ in his self-emptying. As was shown in Chapter 4, Zen speaks of the Great Death and also of dying on the mat, that is, the mat and cushion on which we sit *zazen*. This is the death of the separate ego-self, and in this sense is directly aligned to the baptism of all Christians into the death and resurrection of Christ. From the perspective of Zen, the resurrection life is experienced as that which comes from beyond the ego-self and which we cannot manipulate or make happen ourselves. From the Christian perspective, it is sheer grace, coming from the unfathomable abyss of the Father's love. In this regard, it is possible, therefore, to discern what might be considered to be something of a Trinitarian rhythm and shape, akin to the way in which God is known as the economic Trinity, in the practice of *zazen*.

Reflecting on the practice of Zen more broadly, in terms of emptiness and form, provides a route into understanding Zen in terms of the immanent Trinity. As we have seen, the practice of Zen leads us along a pathless path to the experience of emptiness. This emptiness is the fundamental nature of everything. It is neither nothingness nor vacancy and could just as easily be referred to as fullness. As emptiness, though, it is completely beyond concept, thought or idea. It is an abyss, the unknown and unknowable. At the very same time, though, this emptiness manifests itself and is known as form; form is emptiness and emptiness is form. Emptiness and form are not two – they are the same reality experienced from two perspectives. To awaken to the reality of emptiness as form and form as emptiness, is to awaken to the indivisibility of life, which is experienced as freedom, joy and peace, but, above all, as compassion and love.

There is clearly a resonance here with Trinitarian experience. The Son – form, the known and knowable – reveals the Father – emptiness, the unknown and unknowable – both of whom are completely at one in the love, bliss and joy of the Spirit. As Jesus says: 'Not that anyone has seen the Father except the one who is from God; he has seen the Father' (John 6.46); 'Whoever has seen me has seen the Father' (John 14: 9); and 'It is the Spirit that gives life' (John 6.63). When Jesus invites his disciples to abide in him as he abides in them (John 15.4), he is inviting them and us to awaken to who we are as grounded in a dynamic rhythm of love: as those who are grounded in the emptiness of an unknowable abyss of love, as those who manifest that love in the form of who they are, and as those who are at one with all that is in the bliss and joy of the love and compassion that embraces everyone and everything. Christianity and Zen alike invite us to discover the ultimate – God or the Dharma – as graciousness, compassion and love. When we awaken to this reality, we discover who we are, we realise the true self of all, and we find that we are at home with ourselves.

Summary: being at home with oneself

This chapter has sought to show that at the heart of human aspiration and experience is a desire to be truly who we are, and yet, at the same time, that there is a nervousness borne of our tendency to compare ourselves with others, which inhibits us from being at home with ourselves. This was illustrated with reference, first, to the relationship between Peter and John in John's gospel, and then, second, in relation to Jōshū's monks, the old woman and Jōshū. The interesting thing about Peter is that although he had been the recipient of the unconditional love of the Risen Christ, he was still insecure, the implication being that he needed time to grow into the full awareness of his being accepted as he was then and there.

This was related to the practice of *zazen*, where the experience of having undergone the Great Death was seen to be not entirely dissimilar, in that delusions still remain. The desire to rid oneself of delusions, though, is counter-productive, for what is actually required in order to deprive them of their negative hold on us is a compassionate acceptance of ourselves and others as we are, exactly what the Risen Christ's acceptance of Peter was intended to elicit for him. The key to *zazen* is letting go of thoughts, a disposition described by Dōgen as 'non-thinking'. This practice of non-thinking leads to a profound stillness, silence and peace, to what Christians refer to as God.

It was suggested that the practice of contemplative prayer in the Christian tradition has a remarkable resonance with the practice of *zazen*, as the words of both Meister Eckhart and the anonymous author of *The Cloud of Unknowing* show. For the latter, far surpassing the exercise of thought is the practice of love. It is by love and by love alone that God may be known. This gave rise to a further reflection on the congruence between Zen and the Christian experience of God as Trinity, in which it was suggested that a Trinitarian rhythm and dynamic can be discerned in the practice of *zazen*. This is what Ruben Habito describes as the 'inner circle of mystery', since 'taken together, the elements of the Zen awakened life open our eyes to a "Triune Mystery" that is at the very heart of our human existence' (Habito 2004, p.109):

> One simply awakens to one's True Self as already embedded within the heart of this Mystery: The Unknown, the Manifest and the Sea of Compassion. One awakens as already situated at the inner circle of its dynamic life, from Breath to Breath... To awaken to one's true nature is to realise oneself as embraced in this dynamic circle of Love. It is to recognise one's True Self as the very bosom of this triune Mystery of Love, in every breath, every step, every moment of one's life. (Habito 2004, p.110)

And this is to be at home with ourselves and with all that is.

Chapter 6

At Home in the World

The false division between practice and action

From 2010 to 2014, the BBC broadcast three series of a situation comedy called *Rev*. Its central character was an Anglican priest, the Reverend Adam Smallbone, who had moved from rural ministry in Suffolk to be the vicar of the fictional inner-city parish of St Saviour in the Marshes, Hackney, in East London. Adam finds himself in a situation where the fabric of the church building is in a state of disrepair, where the number of people committed to the life of the church and who regularly attend services is small and dwindling, where for much of the time the Church as a whole is regarded as an irrelevance to most people's lives, and yet where those who have nowhere else to turn to for spiritual or material support make their way inexorably to the door of the vicarage in search of help.

Adam is a priest with a big heart. In the third episode of the first series, he decides to allow a local Muslim group to use the church for teaching and prayer. When the group arrives for the first time, he has just been dealing with the theft of all the lead from the roof of the church, but he manages, nevertheless, to welcome the teacher, Faiza, and her group of a dozen or so children with attentiveness and warmth. As Faiza sets about teaching the children, Adam and his colleague, Nigel, a lay reader – who thinks that he himself should be a vicar, and that, without question, he would be a very much better one than Adam – sit in the wings and observe what goes on. The following conversation ensues:

> Adam: Look how comfortable they are with their religion. It's because Islam's so woven into their everyday lives, whereas for our lot it's just something you do on Sundays, if you can be bothered.

> Nigel: Christian kids are all in the pub taking drugs, because that's more fun than listening to your sermons!

> Adam: Ha, ha, Nigel! Maybe if other people had a grasp of these values, our roof wouldn't be halfway to Beijing. (Hollander and Wood 2010)

Adam's observation that Islam is woven into everyday life is undoubtedly true in theory, but, then, it is also true that Christianity is similarly woven in theory. It is turning the theory into practice that seems to be the problem. Many would, no doubt, recognise more than a degree of truth in Adam's comment that, for those who do go to church, it seems to be a Sunday-only activity for the most part. The reasons for this are far beyond the scope of this book to examine. Much of the responsibility for this state of affairs, though, can probably be laid at the door of the Church itself. Even to this day, encouraging people to grow spiritually and be more committed seems to consist more often than not in persuading them to be more involved in church activities, rather than in enabling them to live out their faith in the world as a whole, whether that be at home, at work, or wherever they find themselves for most of the time when they are not in church. Despite the fact that Christianity celebrates the Incarnation at its heart, through which God is united to the world not just in its religious activities but in the totality of its life, the entirely false division between the 'sacred' and the 'secular' persists in the minds of many.

To be fair to the Church, the reasons for this are complex. One such reason, for example, might well be a kind of success on its own part. Whereas for many centuries, the Church itself was the only provider of such things as education and healthcare, and even then for relatively few, so much has the Church enabled society to see that everyone is entitled to education and healthcare, that the state now sees the responsibility to ensure that all have access to these things as its own. In other words, the state provides what the Church on its own no longer has the means to do, and this, surely, is a good thing. The consequence, however, is that while the Church is certainly still involved in these and many other areas of life, it is no longer necessarily the driving force, and is thus perceived to be at something of a distance rather than at the centre of things.

There are further complications, however. In what is now a much more diverse and pluralistic society than it was, say, just 50 or so years ago, legislation has been brought into effect to ensure that it is not just Christianity which is protected. Laws have come into existence to ensure that a variety of religious and non-religious traditions are held in respect. While it is still generally acknowledged that it is the Christian tradition, rather than any other, which has largely shaped Western culture, Christianity no longer occupies the privileged position to the extent that it once did. Treating others and their worldviews with respect seems to me to be entirely consistent with some of the basic tenets of Christianity itself, such as loving one's neighbour as oneself, and honouring every single person as created in the image and likeness of God, however much one may agree or disagree with, like or dislike them. A negative consequence of respect for diversity, though, is that there can be a reticence among people of all religious traditions in relation to being open about their faith, on the basis of a misguided fear of offending others. For this reason – among others, no doubt – there is a pressure in some quarters to make faith a private matter. In other words, where Christianity is concerned, to keep it as something for Sundays.

The same issue presents itself in Zen, though for different reasons. One of the criticisms of Zen is that, historically, it has not been very much concerned about the causes and conditions of injustice in the world, and with helping to ameliorate things like poverty, in the way that the Church actually has. With its emphasis on seated meditation, and on coming to an acceptance of the way things are in the world, there has, so it seems, been little motivation to make a practical difference to the lives of the many who suffer.

This was brought to my attention when presenting a paper about Zen and Christianity at a conference a while ago.[1] At the end of my presentation, a participant commented that Zen did not seem to be much concerned with changing the world for the better and wondered what resources I thought Zen had to bring to bear on this. My response was to say that central to Zen, as to all Buddhist traditions, is a concern to relieve suffering, and that of direct relevance in this regard are Zen's primary virtues of wisdom and compassion. Such compassion – literally 'suffering with' – undoubtedly requires action of some kind. The challenge, however, is how to act with wisdom; in other words, how to ensure that any action undertaken does not itself arise out of motives of selfishness and egocentricity, and thus add to the suffering it seeks to relieve.

In recent times, this deficiency in the practice of Zen has been in the process of being redressed, not least through its contact with Western culture. The well-known Vietnamese Zen Master, Thich Nhất Hạnh, for example, first put his mind to this in 1993 with the publication of his book, *Interbeing: Fourteen Guidelines for Engaged Buddhism* (2000), since when Zen groups and others have responded to this vision.

One such group is Zen Peacemakers International, which is the most recent iteration of the original vision of its founder, Bernie Tetsugen Glassman Roshi, who first came to be concerned about how Zen could be more socially engaged in the late 1970s and early 1980s. In 1982, Glassman founded Greyston Bakery in Yonkers,

---

1   This paper was adapted and expanded into a chapter for a book (Collingwood 2018, pp.98–117).

USA, with the specific intention of providing employment opportunities for those who found it impossible to get work, particularly the homeless. Since its humble beginnings, it has trained its employees from scratch and developed into a highly successful business with a workforce of some 75 people and an annual turnover of $14 million. Profits are used to fund various not-for-profit sister projects established by Zen Peacemakers International, which now has seventy affiliate centres around the world, and which works with, among others, the homeless, the mentally ill and those who have HIV/AIDS.

What supports and inspires this work are what are called the Three Tenets of Not Knowing, Bearing Witness and Taking Action. Not Knowing refers to the willingness to let go of fixed ideas about ourselves and others, the way we put people and things into boxes, in order to be open to what presents itself at any given moment without clouding it with prejudice and setting up barriers. Bearing Witness is about being open to the totality of life, both its joy and its suffering, including our own prejudices and delusions. Taking Action arises directly out of the practices of Not Knowing and Bearing Witness. It is characterised to a large extent by spontaneity, in the sense that any action is undertaken in response to the totality of situations and circumstances, which are inevitably constantly changing – one of the features of impermanence. This does not result in paralysis or in defaulting to inaction; on the contrary. It is simply that the 'underlying intention is that the action that arises be a caring action, which serves everyone and everything, including yourself, in the whole situation' (Egyoku 2017). The result is action grounded in wisdom and compassion, in which there is no separation between self and other, and which is the unified activity of life unfolding and the true self manifesting itself.[2]

This demonstrates that the division between meditation and action is, of course, an entirely false one. Thich Nhất Hạnh's advocacy of a socially engaged Zen arose directly out of his experience of living through the Vietnam War. For him, meditation that does not then respond to what is happening through action is inauthentic, just as action which is not grounded in meditation runs the risk of losing touch with the roots of wisdom and compassion. Speaking about his experience of meditating during the war, he said:

> You know in Vietnam, when you sat during the war, when you sat in the meditation hall and heard the bombs falling, you had to be aware that the bombs are falling and people are dying. That is part of the practice. Meditation means to be aware of what is happening in the present moment – to your body, to your feelings, to your environment. But if you see and if you don't do anything, where is your awareness? Then where would your enlightenment be? Your compassion? In order not to get lost, you have to be able to continue the practice there, in the midst of all that. But no one can be completely there twenty-four hours a day. I find that after having talked to two or three people who have deep suffering, I, myself feel the need to withdraw in order to recuperate. (Tworkov 1995)

2   Further information about Zen Peacemakers International can be found by visiting the website at https://zenpeacemakers.org. For a flavour of the kind of literature that exists in the area of socially engaged Buddhism, see, for example, Hạnh (2000), Macy (2007, 2013), Murphy (2014), Queen (2001) and Queen & King (1996).

The important thing that is said here relates to the centrality of awareness. Practising *zazen* in a war zone cannot but lead one to be aware of the immense suffering that arises as a result of conflict, as well as of one's own fears and anxieties. At the same time, however, such awareness is practised not only when sitting, but also when meeting those who suffer face to face. Action should inevitably emerge out of that awareness. Given that anyone who practises Zen seriously comes to the realisation sooner or later of the deep interconnectedness of all people and all beings, it follows that when one sits, one is not sitting for oneself alone but for all people and all things. By the same token, in responding to another who is suffering, we are also taking care of our own suffering. There is no separation. This was also a great insight of the apostle Paul, who said, 'If one member suffers, all suffer together with it; if one member is honoured, all rejoice together with it' (1 Corinthians 12.26).

It is the crucial role played by awareness in meditation and action that I wish to expand on in this chapter, for it is this that enables us to be at home in the world and in all that presents itself, however palatable or otherwise. Another way of putting it would be to say that it is awareness that enables us to live in the present moment, to be present to life as it is right now, and it is out of this awareness that action appropriate to the situation arises. In this regard, Christianity and Zen are at one. What follows in this chapter will lead finally to a Zen-informed reading of the well-known parable of the Sheep and the Goats, in the hope of showing that this is so.

Practice is life, life is practice

Many Christians find it difficult to connect what goes on in church with the rest of their lives. For those who practise Zen, there is the opposite danger of getting stuck in emptiness. We have to discover that emptiness manifests itself in this world of form, and that form is essentially empty, as the *Heart Sūtra* puts it. When no one thing is seen to have its own substantial independent existence, we awaken to the fact not that nothing really exists, but that everything is in relationship, indeed that everything *is* relationship. This is partly what the Christian doctrine of God as Trinity seeks to affirm. The very being of God, in whom we 'live, move and have our being' (Acts 17.28), in his whose very image and likeness we are, is relationship. God, and everything to which God gives life, exists as a fundamental communion. The story of the Fall articulates, as we have seen, how our own egocentricity, self-assertiveness and desire to grasp wounds and fractures this essential unity. The biblical story suggests that even work and the tasks of daily living will be experienced as hardship because of the Fall (Genesis 3.17–19).

Hidden away, however, in one of the so-called apocryphal books of the Bible, Sirach or Ecclesiasticus, is a passage that it would be so easy to overlook, and yet which provides the most glorious clue as to how this fracture can be overcome. And it has to do with seeing work as prayer.

The book is about wisdom. 'All wisdom,' it affirms, 'is from the Lord' (Sirach 1.1). About four-fifths of the way through the book, the question is asked as to how artists and craftspeople can acquire wisdom. For the scribe there is no problem, for the scribe has leisure to grow in wisdom, as 'only the one who has little business can become wise'

(Sirach 38.24). This seems to imply that wisdom is possible only for those who are relieved of the need to engage in the everyday tasks of life. If that is really so, the author asks, then how can one who handles the plough, or drives oxen, or cuts the signets of seals, or paints a lifelike image, or works at the anvil, or sits at the potter's wheel, become wise? (Sirach 38.25–30). The author's answer is well worth quoting in full:

> All these rely on their hands,
> and all are skilful in their own work.
> Without them no city can be inhabited, and wherever they live, they will not go hungry.
> Yet they are not sought out for the council of the people,
> nor do they attain eminence in the public assembly.
> They do not sit in the judge's seat,
> nor do they understand the decisions of the courts; they cannot expound discipline or judgement,
> and they are not found among the rulers.
> But they maintain the fabric of the world,
> and their concern is for the exercise of their trade.
> (Sirach 38.31–34a)

I suggested above that the significance of this passage lies in the connection it makes between work and prayer. That connection will as yet be completely obscure. This is because the final line can be translated in one of two ways. The alternative to 'and their concern is for the exercise of their trade' is what makes all the difference: '*and their prayer is in the practice of their trade'.*[3] It is this translation which opens up a whole realm of possibilities.

How, it might be asked, can prayer consist in the practice of trade? It all depends, of course, on the attitude that is brought to bear. I want to suggest that awareness is the clue. If we reflect for a moment on the various trades mentioned in this passage, it should be immediately clear that the successful outcome of each task depends on the quality of attention that is brought to bear on it. Such attention requires an absence of self, which amounts to a complete 'at-one-ness' with the activity. When 'self' intrudes, things go wrong. Thus, the ploughman is 'careful about the fodder for the heifers' (Sirach 38.26b), artisans are 'careful to finish their work' (Sirach 38.27b), the smith's 'eyes are on the pattern of the object' and he 'is careful to complete his decoration' (Sirach 38.28), just as the potter is 'always deeply concerned over his products' and he 'takes care in firing the kiln' (Sirach 38.29–30). What is being highlighted is the quality of attention, which requires a kind of selflessness. It is a kind of 'doing nothing', in the sense that it demands that there is no intrusion of the ego; the ego has to be asleep, so to speak.

For the practice of the trade to be prayer, there has to be an attentiveness and stillness. In Zen terms, this means that the whole activity is really a kind of non-action, in which, through, the union of the worker, the work and the material that is being worked, this is simply the self functioning as the self. When such a quality of attention is

---

3   This is highlighted in *The Holy Bible* (NRSV) (1995) Oxford: Oxford University Press, *The Apocryphal/Deuterocanonical Books of the Old Testament*, p.106,f. The RSV translation opts for the alternative translation, to which I am drawing attention.

brought to bear on whatever we are doing at any time, the activity is, in Christian terms, consecrated, made holy. It becomes what it truly is.

What happens when such attention is absent is all too much part of the experience of all of us. In this regard, our experience of *zazen* and activity alike mutually inform each other. When practising *zazen*, it is a common experience that we can 'take our eye off the ball' – how illuminating a metaphor that is in this context – we become distracted, we get caught up in our thoughts. When we become aware of this, we return to our breath and to 'non-thinking'. This is a practice that can be adopted in any situation. It applies to musicians, sports people, surgeons, train drivers, machine operators, accountants, and so on. When our attention is distracted, errors occur, sometimes bad ones, adding to the suffering of the world. The car driver who momentarily takes his or her eyes off the road, fails to be aware of a child running onto the road to retrieve a ball, with the result that the child is knocked down and killed. The suffering that ensues is not only that of the child but also of his or her family, of the driver, and of others closely or remotely involved. When one suffers, all suffer.

I have often been amazed at how someone like Andy Murray, the British Wimbledon champion, for example, is able to save a succession of three, sometimes four, consecutive match points in tennis. The nerve required to do so is extraordinary. In order to do this, though, the still mind that is experienced in *zazen* is absolutely necessary. When under such pressure, the thinking mind can go into overdrive. The stories we tell about ourselves can be entirely counter-productive, particularly if they are negative. I could imagine something like the following monologue going on in Andy Murray's head: 'You always do this, you idiot. Why don't you ever learn? Here we are again, love 40 down. You're going to lose this one and then you're out of the competition. You're never going to be a really great tennis player.' I suspect that Murray has actually learned how to deal with this sort of thing over time. As is the case with *zazen*, thoughts cannot be suppressed, but we can desist from identifying with them. However much of a fix Murray seems to be in, he appears to be wholly present, wholly attentive to what is happening now. His mind does not seem to be focused on what has just occurred or on what might happen. This is what enables him to save matches in the way he does.

The same would apply just as much to positive stories that he might tell himself, though. If he were to approach a situation of being love 40 down by assuming that he could win the point easily, or by telling himself that he always gets himself out of such scrapes and comes back from the brink, complacency would set in and, as a result, his attention would slacken, almost certainly with disastrous consequences.

In what I have described so far, I have been suggesting that any activity can be the occasion for practice. This is very much the message of the Zen Master Ichu, as Charlotte Joko Beck recounts:

A student said to Master Ichu, 'Please write for me something of great wisdom.' Master Ichu picked up his brush and wrote one word: 'Attention.' The student said, 'Is that all?' The master wrote, 'Attention. Attention.' The student became irritable. 'That doesn't seem profound or subtle to me.' In response, Master Ichu wrote simply,

'Attention. Attention. Attention.' In frustration, the student demanded, 'What does this word attention mean?' Master Ichu replied, 'Attention means attention'. (Beck 1993, p.168)

The point of the story is that everything comes down to a matter of giving attention. When we are wholly absorbed in whatever it is to which we are giving attention, we experience what Dōgen calls the dropping away of body and mind, the reality of no-self, and we awaken to ten thousand things. We realise that we are not separate from anyone or anything, that our self is, in fact, all that is. In this state of awareness, we realise that there is no separation, no division, neither between meditation and action, nor anything else, for all is the seamless functioning of the self. This is our natural, original state. So, with this in mind, let us turn now to see how this might inform our understanding of Jesus' parable of the Sheep and the Goats (Matthew 25.31–46).

The parable of the Sheep and the Goats

The gist of the parable will probably be known to many. It envisages a judgement at the end of time, when the Son of Man comes in glory. All the nations will be gathered before him and then separated as a shepherd separates sheep from goats. The only criterion as to whether people are saved is whether they have responded to the needs of those who suffer. Thus, to those on his right he says:

Come, you that are blessed by my Father, inherit the kingdom prepared for you from the foundation of the world; for I was hungry and you gave me food, I was thirsty and you gave me something to drink, I was a stranger and you welcomed me, I was naked and you gave me clothing, I was sick and you took care of me, I was in prison and you visited me. (Matthew 25.34–36)

The rather surprising reaction of those who are thus saved is not one of pure and unadulterated joy, but sheer incomprehension. They have absolutely no recollection of having come to the aid of anyone:

Lord, when was it that we saw you hungry and gave you food, or thirsty and gave you something to drink? And when was it that we saw you a stranger and welcomed you, or naked and gave you clothing? And when was it that we saw you sick or in prison and visited you? (Matthew 25.37–39)

The Son of Man, who is now referred to as the king, says to them: 'Truly I tell you, just as you did it to one of the least of these who are members of my family, you did it to me' (Matthew 25.40).

The king then tells those who have been divided to the left that they are accursed, because when he was hungry, they gave him no food, when he was thirsty, they gave him nothing to drink. When he was a stranger, they did not welcome him, when he was naked, he was not clothed, and when he was sick and in prison, he was left unvisited by them. At this, those who are being sent into eternal punishment protest strongly that they are totally unaware of ever having seen the king hungry or thirsty or naked or sick or in prison, to which the king replies: 'Truly I tell you, just as you did not do it to the least of these, you did not do it to me' (Matthew 25.45).

In many ways, this probably seems about as far away from Zen as you could get. It is thoroughly dualistic, with division and judgement being the whole point of the parable. And yet, when read in a purely Christian context alone, there are some perplexing features of the story. The outcome of the judgement is salvation, and the only criterion for salvation is whether people respond to those who are in need. On this basis, it would be fairly understandable that those who simply do not see need and the suffering that goes with it should be treated harshly, but what account is to be given of those who actually met the criterion without being aware of it? What, it might be asked, is the merit in that?

Furthermore, it is to be noted that the king – Christ, we might reasonably be expected to assume – is wholly identified with the needs of the suffering. Indeed, it is asserted in the story that he *is* those who suffer: 'Truly I tell you, just as you did it to one of the least of these who are members of my family, you did it to *me*', and conversely, 'Truly I tell you, just as you did not do it to the least of these, you did not do it to *me*'. In a thoroughly dualistic parable, then, we also have an affirmation of non-duality. What are we to make of this? Is this a contradiction? Is it just a sloppy story? Are we, indeed, not to worry too much about this? In this matter, Zen can be of considerable help in enabling us to get to the heart of the parable, for I want to suggest that this is a story primarily about enlightenment.

Pre-awakening, awakening and post-awakening

The help that comes from Zen derives from an understanding of what unawakened and awakened states are. This is captured in a Zen proverb: 'Before enlightenment, chop wood and carry water. After enlightenment, chop wood and carry water.' This is likely to be as perplexing as the parable of the Sheep and Goats, for it seems to imply that the unawakened and awakened states are identical. A saying of Ch'ing Yűan (1067–1120) can help us to read between the lines a little here:

> Before I had studied Zen for thirty years, I saw mountains as mountains, and waters as waters. When I arrived at a more intimate knowledge, I came to the point where I saw that mountains are not mountains, and waters are not waters. But now that I have got its very substance I am at rest. For it's just that I see mountains once again as mountains, and waters once again as waters. (Watts 1957, p.115)

In his *Mountains and Waters Sūtra*, Dōgen says something very similar, but the way he expresses it is as opaque as the proverb: 'An ancient Buddha said, "Mountains are mountains, waters are waters." These words do not mean mountains are mountains; they mean mountains are mountains' (Tanahashi 1995, p.107).

What is being referred to here in a very condensed form is a transition from an unawakened state of mind to an awakened one. From the vantage point of the unawakened state, things seem to be just what they appear to be: mountains look like mountains and waters look like waters. If anyone whose perspective this is were to be asked what they saw when they looked at a mountain, they would probably reply, rather incredulously, that they saw nothing but a mountain, as if to say that it was perfectly obvious that it was so, and that there could not possibly be another way of seeing it. This unawakened state is one of separation, division and duality. Everything seems to be other, and the centre of reference is the individual self. It is only when the desire for enlightenment, when the Bodhi Mind is raised – almost always as a result of experiencing suffering – that we are likely to experience the beginning of a transition. Until then, life is experienced as opposition, with everything in conflict. The reality, however, is that we are unaware of the contribution that we might make to that conflict.

The second stage of this transition is where our delusions begin to be seen for what they are. In particular, we realise that our egocentricity leads to a deluded or skewed way of seeing things. Separation, division and duality are no longer the order of the day. Instead, as the grip on the self is weakened and loosed, the sense that everything has its own substantial independent existence falls away. As has been noted above, this is what Dōgen describes as the dropping away of body and mind. This constitutes an awakening to emptiness.

Here is the curious twist, though. It is precisely as we realise that things do not have a separate existence that we come to appreciate all things in their uniqueness, in what Zen often describes as 'suchness'. This means what might be called 'things as they are'. As I have stated on several occasions throughout the book, emptiness is not vacancy or nothingness, but interconnectedness and interrelatedness.

In this final stage, then, nothing is seen to have substantial independent existence and yet everything is just as it is. In other words, the three stages are: mountains are mountains, mountains are not mountains, mountains are not mountains but they are mountains.

This is exactly what is experienced in *zazen*. When we first begin to practise, we are likely to have a very strong sense of ourselves as an individual self. There will be many reasons why we may have been led to start sitting at all, one of them being the sense, perhaps, that there is something more to life, something that we are missing, or something that is unsatisfactory. This is what constitutes the experience of life as *duḥkha*. Suffering invariably strengthens the sense of the separateness of the individual self. It is me suffering. We are aware of our delusion.

The practice of letting go of thoughts and of all that arises in the mind, of everything that creates a sense of a separate self, as we sit, gradually dissolves the barriers, and the self gives way to no-self, or emptiness. This can be a blissful state and the temptation is to long for this every time we sit. At this stage, delusions have come to be seen as not having the grip on us that they once did, and yet when we continue to be aware of their presence every time we sit *zazen*, we still experience them as something that should no longer be there. The desire for them to be gone is itself a form of craving, which has to be surrendered.

The paradox, then, is that it is only by accepting ourselves as we are, as being essentially empty and yet embracing our delusions, that enlightenment and delusion are no longer experienced as being in opposition to each other. Enlightenment is to experience things just as they are. Thus to employ what was said in relation to mountains above, and risk being incredibly convoluted and verbose, something like the following has to be said. In the first stage, enlightenment is enlightenment and delusion is delusion. In the second stage, enlightenment is not enlightenment, and delusion is not delusion. In the third stage, enlightenment is enlightenment, and delusion is delusion, but enlightenment is not enlightenment and delusion is not delusion. This is what the proverb, 'Before enlightenment, chop wood and carry water. After enlightenment, chop wood and carry water', is really getting at. To all intents and purposes, 'before' and 'after' look exactly the same, but it would be more accurate to say that they are both the same and different.

Reading the Sheep and the Goats in the light of Zen

I want to suggest that all this can help us to approach the parable of the Sheep and the Goats in a way that might make sense of some of the apparent oddities and anomalies. Before proceeding, however, I need to make it clear what I am and what I am not saying. Historically speaking, Zen and Christianity are clearly different traditions. I am not saying, therefore, that the parable shows influence of Zen teaching or inspiration. As far as I am aware, there is no such evidence, although I have suggested that there is a definite affinity between Zen and some of Jesus' teachings.[4] Nor am I proposing that the tripartite scheme outlined above, in relation to mountains, chopping wood and carrying water, can be imposed without remainder on to the parable. It cannot. What I am suggesting,

---

4   See Chapter 2.

though, is that the insights of Zen can be applied to the parable in such a way that might enable the parable to be read with fresh eyes, in the hope of making sense of some of the perplexities that the text presents on its own terms. The key to this, as I stated above, lies in the notion of awareness.

The most baffling thing about the parable is that neither the sheep on the right, nor the goats on the left, seem to have any awareness that they were encountering Christ himself in those they came across. The sheep are commended for doing the right thing, and yet they are completely unaware of having done so. The goats are condemned for not having done the right thing, and yet neither are they aware. To all intents and purposes, it looks as if they conduct themselves in exactly the same way, yet one group is praised and the other is judged harshly. What is it that makes the difference? For this is not unlike chopping wood and carrying water, or seeing mountains as mountains, and then seeing them not as mountains, but then seeing them as mountains and not as mountains again. What is the difference between the first and the last states?

It all has to do with self and no-self or true self. Let us begin with the goats. The significant thing is not so much that they did not see Christ, but that they did not see anyone other than themselves at all, let alone anyone in need. They did not feed the hungry or give drink to the thirsty, nor did they welcome the stranger or clothe the naked or visit those in prison. They were, it must be assumed, completely wrapped up in themselves. Indeed, their perspective was coloured entirely by self. This represents a deluded state, one characterised by a complete lack of awareness. Being so preoccupied with themselves, they were blinded even to the presence of others, especially as suffering beings. Their state was one of dullness and clouded perception.

In this regard, we are probably no different from them in one way or another. We all know what it is to be preoccupied with ourselves, with our own commitments and concerns, to see everything from our own narrow, individual perspective alone. We become shut in on and enclosed within ourselves. Basic awareness and empathy are lacking and we fail to perceive that our own well-being – our salvation – is not an individual matter but is bound up with that of everyone and everything else. The sense of separation is itself part of the delusion, and it is only when the suffering of others impinges on us that we are awakened to a wider and broader awareness and broken out of self-centredness.

When this happens, we awaken to the fact that the range of compassion is actually infinite, and the first stage in this is both to awaken to the fact of the suffering of others, and also to awaken to the fact that they are more than who we think they are. They are not just beings who suffer but Christ himself, present in all things and in all people. Part of responding to the suffering of others is to want to come to their assistance, but there is a danger that we can do so and yet still fail to see that they and we are not separate. If we think that compassion consists in our doing good to others, we can be easily disabused of any such idea, if we reflect on any occasions when we might have been the object of someone doing good to us. Such action, though often well motivated, has the effect of actually asserting the unconscious or even conscious superiority of the other, and of being patronising towards us, thus strengthening the sense of separation. Even in seeking to meet others with compassion, this can still be motivated by a strong sense of 'I', which falls short of real compassion by asserting a separate individual identity.

We are one humanity and one creation. It is the belief in and assertion of separateness which leads to suffering, and Christ is completely at one with the whole of creation in its suffering. The passage where the apostle Paul affirms that where one suffers, all suffer, is actually about the Body of Christ. He draws attention to the fact that there is only one body, albeit with different members, each with their respective functions. There is something ludicrous about the eye, the ear, the nose, the hand or the foot wanting to go it alone, and yet this is exactly what we seek to do. We separate ourselves from the whole.

In the parable of the Sheep and the Goats, Christ is identified with the whole – what you did or did not do, you did or did not do to me. The whole creation is the Body of Christ, which, as Paul says elsewhere, 'groans with eager longing for the revealing of the children of God' (Romans 8.19). The goats fell short in failing to see, first, that there were others in the picture in addition to themselves, and, second, that these others were actually Christ himself – all of them. We all share a common delusion with them, but this is something which is brought to light and transformed every time Christians celebrate the Eucharist. The bread and wine, when placed on the altar represent the whole creation, in all its creativity, suffering and potential. Most Christians would want to affirm that in one way or another the bread and wine become the Body and Blood of Christ. The more pressing question, perhaps, is how not just the Church, but the whole of humanity and all creation, is enabled to realise its true identity as the Body of Christ.

The Church is not separate from the rest of humanity or creation, as if the eye were separate from the body. Together we are all already that body; we simply do not see it.

The goats, then, have to awaken from a state in which they are like the eye that does not see itself as part of the body, to one where it is aware of the body alone, which is none other than Christ himself. Where do the sheep fit in to all this, then? We should remind ourselves that just like the goats, they did not see Christ either, and yet they were commended for attending to those in need and, in so doing, for attending to Christ. How can this difference be explained, for outwardly neither the sheep nor the goats were aware of Christ? One important feature makes all the difference, though, and that is that in the case of the sheep, the hungry were indeed fed, the thirsty were given something to drink, the stranger was welcomed, the naked were fed, and those in prison were visited. Whether they realised it or not, the sheep were doing what was necessary.

This can be explained not as sheer luck but as something far more profound. If the goats were so full of self that they could not see any other being at all, the sheep were so empty of self, that there was no self to be conscious of, or, as we are more accustomed to saying, no self-consciousness. What they did was so natural that they were no longer aware of self and other; there was only unself-conscious action itself. This point is made very well in a *kōan*, Case 89, from *The Blue Cliff Record*, entitled: *The Hand and Eyes of the Great Bodhisattva of Compassion.*

> Yun Yen asked Tao Wu: 'What does the Bodhisattva of Great Compassion use so many hands and eyes for?' Wu said: 'It's like someone reaching back groping for a pillow

in the middle of the night.' Yen said: 'I understand.' Wu said: 'How do you understand it?' Yen said: 'All over the body are hands and eyes.' Wu said: 'You have said quite a bit there, but you've only said eighty percent of it.' Yen said: 'What do you say, Elder Brother?' Wu said: 'Throughout the body are hands and eyes'. (Cleary & Cleary 2013, p.489)

It has been suggested that Yun Yen and Tao Wu were brothers, although it might well be that they were simply brother monks. In the exchange that takes place between them, Yun Yen asks Tao Wu about the Bodhisattva of Great Compassion, otherwise known as Guānyīn or Kannon or Kanzeon or Avalokiteśwara, the archetype of compassion. Depicted as either male or female or even androgynous, Guānyīn is known as the one with a thousand arms and a thousand eyes, hence Yun Yen's question: What are all these hands and eyes used for? Wu, it will be noticed, appears not to answer the question, but says that it is like someone reaching out to adjust the position of a pillow while asleep in bed at night. When he asks Yun Yen what his understanding is, he replies that the hands and eyes cover the whole of the body. Wu declares that he is about 80 per cent correct. When Yun Yen challenges Wu for his understanding, Wu states that the hands and eyes do not simply cover the body, but that the whole body is hands and eyes in every part.

If we reflect for a moment on what it is like to change position in bed in the middle of the night, we should probably conclude that we do not really analyse the situation before deciding what to do about the pillow. Most of the time we may not even be aware of changing position or adjusting the pillow; we do it without thinking. It is as if our body just knows what to do naturally and performs the task quite spontaneously and without a moment's thought. Just as the hand reaches out for the pillow, so are acts of compassion a spontaneous and natural reaching out. When Wu tells Yun Yen that he has got the answer only 80 per cent right, because the hands and eyes are not just all over the body on the outside but through and through, he is really saying that every fibre of our being is shot through with compassion, which, in the truly awakened state, acts without thinking. There is no consciousness of self or other, just the unity of action.

This, I want to suggest, is the state in which the sheep find themselves, and is why they are commended for their action. Their action is so spontaneous that they are not even aware of the need, let alone of the other person, or that it is Christ. In this regard, their action is like that of reaching out in the night to adjust a pillow. It is done without thinking. It is simply compassion – Christ – hands and eyes through and through, being and doing what compassion is and does. It is our natural, awakened, enlightened state.

Reading the parable of the Sheep and the Goats in the light of Zen can enable us to overcome some of the difficulties inherent in the text itself. The symbol of Guānyīn can remind us of the traps involved in making an abstraction, an idea, a concept of the self, which, in the final analysis, only get in the way of reality and separate us from our lived and embodied experience. To awaken to our own enlightenment is to be aware of the essential unity of all things, in which each thing is just what it is – the manifestation of wisdom and compassion.

Summary: at home with life

This chapter began by suggesting that Zen and Christianity alike tend to experience an imbalance between practice and action, which obscures their essential unity. Zen has historically underplayed action and engagement rather than *zazen*, although it should be abundantly clear by now that any choice between meditation and action is a fundamentally false one. Christianity, however, has been second to none, arguably, in social action. The problem, still faced by many Christians today, is that what takes place in church on a Sunday and the tasks and demands of everyday life often seem unconnected. Our experience of ourselves and of life as a whole is thus, to a degree, schizophrenic. Our natural, enlightened state is not one of division and separation but of non-dual communion. This should not be imagined to be some special state, though. It is simply us and all beings being who and what we are, functioning as the one true self. If there is anything special about it at all, it is the astonishing realisation that, on the one hand, everything is ordinary, but, on the other, everything is extraordinary, and that, further still, everything is both ordinary and extraordinary at the same time. When we awaken to this, we are not simply at home in the world, we at home with the whole of life, for the whole of life is what we are.

References

Abels, J.J. (2012) *Making Zen Your Own; Giving Life to Twelve Key Golden Age Ancestors*. Boston, MA: Wisdom Publications.

Abhishiktānanda [Henri le Saux] (1975) *The Further Shore*. Delhi: ISPCK (Indian Society for Promoting Christian Knowledge).

Abhishiktānanda [Henri le Saux] (1976) *Hindu-Christian Meeting Point*. Delhi: ISPCK.

Abhishiktānanda [Henri le Saux] (1984) *Saccidananda: A Christian Approach to Advaitic Experience*. Delhi: ISPCK.

Alter, R. (2007) *The Book of Psalms: A Translation with Commentary*. New York, NY & London: W.W. Norton & Company.

Armstrong, K. (2000) *Buddha*. London: Phoenix.

Beck, C.J. (1993) *Nothing Special: Living Zen*. New York, NY: Harper Collins.

Becket, L. (1981) *Richard Wagner: Parsifal*. Cambridge: Cambridge University Press.

Bell, R. (2013) *Wagner's Parsifal: An Appreciation in the Light of his Theological Journey*. Eugene, OR: Cascade Books.

Bodhi, B. (trans.) (1997) *Discourses of the Ancient Nuns*. Kandy: Buddhist Publication Society. Accessed on 26/02/18 at www.accesstoinsight. org/lib/authors/bodhi/bl143.html

Brown Hedgpeth, N. (2013) 'The Old Woman of Mount Wutai.' In Z.F. Caplow & R.S. Moon (eds) *The Hidden Lamp: Stories from Twenty-Five Centuries of Awakened Women*. Boston, MA: Wisdom Publications.

Caplow, Z.F. & Moon, R.S. (eds) (2013) *The Hidden Lamp: Stories from Twenty-Five Centuries of Awakened Women*. Boston, MA: Wisdom Publications.

Cassian, J. (trans. Luibheid, C.) (1985) *Conferences*. New York, NY: Paulist Press.

Cleary, T. & Clearly, J.C. (trans.) (2013) *The Blue Cliff Record*. Boston, MA & London: Shambhala.

Collingwood, C. (2018) 'No Peace among the Nations without Peace among the Religions: How the Experience of Christian–Buddhist Dialogue Could Help to Build Peace among Religions and Nations.' In P. Kollontai, S. Yore & S. Kim (eds) *The Role of Religion in Peacebuilding: Crossing the Boundaries of Prejudice and Distrust*. London: Jessica Kingsley Publishers.

Cook, F.D. (2002) *How to Raise an Ox: Zen Practice as Taught in Master Dogen's Shobogenzo* (Essays and Translations). Boston, MA: Wisdom Publications.

Cook, F.D. (trans.) (2003) *The Record of Transmitting the Light: Zen Master Keizan's Denkoroku*. Boston, MA: Wisdom Publications.

Cornille, C. (ed.) (2010) *Many Mansions? Multiple Religious Belonging and Christian Identity*. Eugene, OR: Wipf and Stock.

Cottingham, J., Stoothoff, R. & Murdoch, D. (eds) (1984) *The Philosophical Writings of Descartes Volume II*. Cambridge: Cambridge University Press.

Cottingham, J., Stoothoff, R. & Murdoch, D. (eds) (1985) *The Philosophical Writings of Descartes Volume I*. Cambridge: Cambridge University Press.

Davies, O. (trans.) (1994) *Meister Eckhart: Selected Writings*. Harmondsworth: Penguin Books.

Dōgen, E. & Uchiyama, K. (2005) *How to Cook Your Life: From the Zen Kitchen to Enlightenment* (trans. Wright, T.) Boston, MA: Shambhala.

Drew, R. (2011) *Buddhist and Christian? An Exploration of Dual Belonging*. London & New York, NY: Routledge.

du Boulay, S. (1998) *Beyond the Darkness: A Biography of Bede Griffiths*. London: Rider.

Dumoulin, H. (2005a) *Zen Buddhism: A History – Volume One: India and China*. Bloomington, IN: World Wisdom.

Dumoulin, H. (2005b) *Zen Buddhism: A History – Volume Two: Japan.* Bloomington, IN: World Wisdom.

Egyoku, W.N. (2017) 'Hold to the Center: Zen Advice for when Things Blow up around You.' *Tricycle: The Buddhist Review*, Summer 2017. Accessed on 15/03/18 available by subscription at: https://tricycle.org/magazine/hold-to-the-center

Eliot, T.S. (2004, first published 1969) *The Complete Poems & Plays.* London: Faber & Faber.

Endō, S. (1996, first published 1969) *Silence* (trans. Johnson, W.) London: Peter Owen (original work published in Japanese in 1966).

Epstein, M. (2013a) *The Trauma of Everyday Life.* London: Hay House.

Epstein, M. (2013b) 'What Changes? Psychotherapy, Buddhism, and a Sense of Boundless Support.' *Tricycle: The Buddhist Review*, Fall 2013. Accessed on 09/02/18 available by subscription at: https://tricycle.org/magazine/what-changes

Ferguson, A. (2011) *Zen's Chinese Heritage: The Masters and their Teachings.* Somerville MA: Wisdom Publications.

Flannery, A. (2014) *Vatican Council II: The Basic Sixteen Documents – Constitutions, Decrees, Declarations.* Collegeville MN: Liturgical Press.

Ford, J.I. (2006) *Zen Master Who? A Guide to the People and Stories of Zen.* Boston MA: Wisdom Publications.

Gombrich, R. (2009) *What the Buddha Thought.* Sheffield: Equinox.

Griffiths, B. (1976) *Return to the Centre.* London: Fount.

Griffiths, B. (1982) *The Marriage of East and West.* London: Collins.

Griffiths, B. (1991) *Vedanta and Christian Faith.* Clearlake CA: Dawn Horse Press.

Gu, G. (2016) *Passing through the Gateless Barrier: Kōan Practice for Real Life.* Boulder, CO: Shambhala.

Habito, R.L.F. (2004) *Living Zen, Loving God.* Boston, MA: Wisdom Publications.

Habito, R.L.F. (2013) *Zen and the Spiritual Exercises.* Maryknoll, NY: Orbis.

Habito, R.L.F. (2017) *Be Still and Know: Zen and the Bible.* Maryknoll, NY: Orbis.

Hạnh, T.N. (2000) *Interbeing: Fourteen Guidelines for Engaged Buddhism*. New Delhi: Full Circle.

Hollander, T. and Wood, J. (2010) *Rev* (series one), London: Big Talk Productions (for the BBC).

Johnston, W. (1970) *The Still Point: Reflections on Zen and Christian Mysticism*. New York, NY: Fordham University Press.

Johnston, W. (1971) *Christian Zen*. New York, NY & London: Harper Colophon Books.

Johnston, W. (1978) *The Inner Eye of Love: Mysticism and Religion*. London: William Collins Sons & Co.

Johnston, W. (1981) *The Mirror Mind: Spirituality and Transformation*. London: William Collins Sons & Co.

Julian of Norwich (1966) *Revelations of Divine Love* (trans. Wolters, C.). Harmondsworth: Penguin.

Keating, T. (1986) *Open Mind, Open Heart: The Contemplative Dimension of the Gospel*. New York, NY: Amity House.

Keating, T. (1987) *The Mystery of Christ: The Liturgy as Christian Experience*. Shaftesbury: Element.

Keating, T. (1992) *Invitation to Love: The Way of Christian Contemplation*. Shaftesbury: Element.

Kennedy, R. (2004) *Zen Gifts to Christians*. London & New York, NY: Continuum.

Kennedy, R. (2007 [1995]) *Zen Spirit, Christian Spirit*. London & New York, NY: Continuum.

Keyes, R. (2011) 'Hokusai Says.' In M. Williams & D. Penman *Mindfulness: A Practical Guide to Finding Peace in a Frantic World*. London: Piatkus.

Kienzle, U. (2010) 'Parsifal and Religion: A Christian Music Drama?' In W. Kinderman & K. Syer (eds) *A Companion to Wagner's Parsifal*. Woodbridge: Boydell & Brewer.

Kim, H-J. (2004) *Eihei Dōgen: Mystical Realist*. Boston, MA: Wisdom Publications.

Loori, J.D. (1996) *The Heart of Being*. Boston MA: Charles E. Tuttle Company.

MacInnes, E. (1999) *Light Sitting in Light: A Christian's Experience of Zen*. Manila: Zen Center for Oriental Spirituality in the Philippines.

MacInnes, E. (2003) *Zen Contemplation for Christians*. Oxford: Sheed & Ward.

Macy, J. (2007) *World as Lover, World as Self: Courage for Global Justice and Ecological Renewal*. Berkeley, CA: Parallax Press.

Macy, J. (2013) *Greening of the Self*. Berkeley, CA: Parallax Press.

Main, J. (1980) *Word into Silence*. London: Darton, Longman & Todd.

Main, J. (1984) *Moment of Christ: The Path of Meditation*. London: Darton, Longman & Todd.

Main, J. (1985) *The Present Christ: Further Steps in Meditation*. London: Darton, Longman & Todd.

Mastrogiovanni, J.L. (2014) *Parsifal: The Will and Redemption – Exploring Wagner's Final Treatise*. North Charleston, SC: CreateSpace Independent Publishing Platform.

McDaniel, R.B. (2016) *Catholicism and Zen*. Richmond Hill, ON: The Sumeru Press.

McGilchrist, I. (2010) *The Master and his Emissary*. New Haven, CT & London: Yale University Press.

McKenty, N. (1986) *In the Stillness Dancing: The Journey of John Main*. London: Darton, Longman & Todd.

Masunaga, R. (1971) *A Primer of Sōtō Zen: A Translation of Dōgen's Shōbōgenzō Zuimonki*. Honolulu: University of Hawaii Press.

Mumon (trans. Anon.) (2006) *The Gateless Gate: All 48 Koans with Commentary by Ekai, called Mumon*. West Valley City, UT: Waking Lion Press.

Murphy, S. (2014) *Minding the Earth, Mending the World: Zen and the Art of Planetary Crisis*. Berkeley, CA: Counterpoint.

Puhl, L.J. (trans.) (1951) *The Spiritual Exercises of St Ignatius*. Chicago, IL: Loyola University Press.

Queen, C. (2001) *Engaged Buddhism in the West*. Somerville MA: Wisdom Publications.

Queen, C. & King, S. (1996) *Engaged Buddhism: Buddhist Liberation Movements in Asia*. New York, NY: Albany State University Press.

Samy, A.M.A. (2009) *The Zen Way*. Dindigul: Vaigarai.

Samy, A.M.A. (2010) *Zen: Ancient and Modern*. Dindigul: Vaigarai.

Samy, A.M.A. (2012) *Zen: The Great Way has No Gates*. Dindigul: Vaigarai.

Samy, A.M.A. (2016) *Zen: Fragrant Blossoms, Falling Grasses*. Perumalmalai: Bodhi Zendo.

Samy, A.M.A. (2017) *Zen: Do Not Linger Where the Buddha Dwells*. Perumalmalai: Bodhi Zendo.

Schofield, P. (2007) *The Redeemer Reborn: Parsifal as the Fifth Opera of Wagner's Ring*. New York, NY: Amadeus Press.

Scorsese, M. (2017) *Silence* [DVD]. Paris: StudioCanal.

Shibayama, Z. (2000) *The Gateless Barrier: Zen comments on the Mumonkan* (trans. Kudo, S.). Boston MA: Shambhala.

Shinoda, M. (1971) *Silence* [DVD]. London: Eureka Entertaniment Ltd., Masters of Cinema.

Strong, J.S. (2001) *The Buddha*. Oxford: Oneworld.

Suzuki, S. (1999) *Zen Mind, Beginner's Mind*. London & Boston, MA: Weatherhill.

Suzuki, S. (2011) 'Commentary.' In B. Nishiari, S. Susuki & K. Uchiyama (trans. Okamura, S., Tanahashi, K., Weitsman, S.M. & Wenger, D.M.) *Dōgen's Genjo Koan: Three Commentaries*. Berkeley, CA: Counterpoint.

Tanahashi, K. (ed.) (1995*) Moon in a Dewdrop: Writings of Zen Master Dogen*. New York, NY: North Point Press.

Toomey, S. (2015) *The Saffron Road: A Journey with Buddha's Daughters*. London: Portobello Books.

Tworkov, H. (1995) 'Interbeing with Thich Nhat Hanh: An Interview.' *Tricycle: The Buddhist Review*, Fall 1995. Accessed on 15/03/18 available by subscription at: https://tricycle.org/magazine/interbeing-thich-nhat-hanh-interview

Ucerler, M.A.J. (2016) 'Martin Scorsese brings "Silence" to the big Screen: A Story of Faith and Betrayal in 17th Century Japan.' *The Huffington Post*, 25/12/2016. Accessed on 30/01/18 available at: www.huffingtonpost.com/entry/martin-scorsese-brings-silence-to-the-big-screen_us_58607807e4b068764965bd45

Uchiyama, K. (1997) *The Wholehearted Way: A Translation of Eihei Dōgen's Bendōwa with commentary by Kōshō Uchiyama Roshi* (trans. Okumura, S. & Leighton, T.D.). North Clarendon, VT: Tuttle Publishing.

Wagner, R. (1962) *Parsifal: Music Drama in Three Acts*. Milwaukee WI: G. Schirmer Inc (libretto trans. Robb, S.).

Watts, A. (1957) *The Way of Zen*. New York, NY: Vintage Books.

Wick, J.S. (2005) *The Book of Equanimity: Illuminating Zen Kōans*. Boston MA: Wisdom Publications.

Williams, M. (2017) 'Martin Scorsese's Silence: He has been faithful to Shusaku Endo's text and to the deep questions within it.' *The Independent*, Monday 9 January 2017. Accessed 30/01/18 at: www.independent.co.uk/arts-entertainment/films/features/martin-scorsese-silence-film-end-sh-saku-novel-adaptation-a7518086.html

Wolters, C. (trans.) (1961) *The Cloud of Unknowing*. Harmondsworth: Penguin Books.

Yamada, K. (trans. with commentary) (2004) *The Gateless Gate: The Classic Book of Zen Kōans*. Boston MA: Wisdom Publications.

Yamada, K. (2015) *Zen: The Authentic Gate*. Somerville MA: Wisdom Publications.

Subject Index

Author Index